The Just In Case Plan

Smart Strategies for Long Term Care Family Conversations and Legacy Protection

by Sherri Combs

Senior Advocate | CEO Silver Streak Senior Services | Author | Aging Systems Strategist | Founder Silver Streak Senior Solutions 501c3 | Public Speaker

The Just in Case Plan
Smart Strategies for Long-Term Care* Family Conversations and Legacy Protection

Published by Silver Streak Publishing
900 Bluemound Rd. Suite 144 PMB 103
Fort Worth, TX 76131

ISBN: 979-8-9944809-0-8 (Soft Cover)
ISBN: 979-8-9944809-2-2 (Epub)
Library of Congress Control Number: 2026904453
Cover Design: Sherri L. Combs
Interior Formatting: Dave Vasudevan
Copyright 2026 Silver Streak Brands LLC

Table of Contents

What others are saying about The Just In Case Plan™

A Compassionate, Practical Guide Every Family Needs, Before Crisis Hits

The Just-In-Case Plan is one of the most honest, practical, and human books I've ever read about aging, long-term care, and family planning. What makes it exceptional is that it doesn't rely on fear, legal jargon, or abstract theory. Instead, Sherri Combs meets readers exactly where they are with clarity, empathy, and real-world wisdom.

This book explains *what actually happens* when families wait too long to plan and more importantly, how to avoid the chaos, conflict, and loss of choice that so many families experience. The real stories are powerful without being overwhelming, and the guidance is clear without being prescriptive. You don't feel judged for what you haven't done yet; you feel supported in taking the next right step.

One of the most valuable aspects of this book is how it bridges emotional reality with practical execution. It addresses not just documents and systems, but dignity, autonomy, family dynamics, and the conversations most people don't know how to start. The "just in case" framing alone is worth the read—it lowers defenses and opens doors that fear usually slams shut.

This is not a book you read once and shelve. It's a resource you return to as life evolves. Whether you are caring for aging parents, planning for your own future, or working professionally with families, **this book should be required reading**.

I truly wish I had this guide earlier in my own life. It would have saved time, stress, and heartache. I'm grateful it exists now and I'll be recommending it to everyone I care about.

-Patty Farmer

Marketing Media & Money Expert, Business Growth Strategist & Coach. International Speaker, Podcast Host, and Magazine Publisher. Owner of M3 Creative Marketing.

Foreword

By Karen Stawicki

Karen is the Co-owner of Compass Financial. Over 30 years of Strategic Expertise in Wealth Management and Co Author of The Power of Three.

Some books teach.
Some books comfort.
And once in a while, a book does both.

Just in Case is one of those rare books.

I read it in one sitting, not because it is short, but because it is sincere, practical, and deeply human. Page after page, Sherri Combs reminds us of something we too often forget in the rush of life: aging is not a problem to solve, but a season to honor.

This book is a beautiful collection of heartwarming stories, honest realities, and gentle guidance. It speaks to the quiet fears that so many aging adults carry but rarely voice, the fear of being a burden, of no longer being useful, of slowly disappearing from the center of family life. Sherri doesn't look away from those emotions. She names them, respects them, and then offers a path forward.

What makes *Just in Case* so special is not only what Sherri says, but how she says it. Her words are compassionate without being sentimental, practical without being cold. She understands that love alone does not always give us the language we need to have hard conversations. This book becomes that language.

Sherri shows us how to gently open doors to conversations we often avoid:

- How to talk with aging parents about the future without fear or defensiveness
- How to guide them when they feel lost, forgotten, or unsure of their purpose
- How to prepare, just in case, without taking away dignity or independence

These are not easy topics. But they are necessary ones. And Sherri approaches them with grace, respect, and a deep belief that no one should walk this season alone.

You can feel her heart on every page. She truly sees the aging, not as fragile or finished, but as valuable, wise, and worthy of care, choice, and dignity. And she writes not only for those who are aging, but for the sons, daughters, spouses, and friends who love them.

Just in Case is more than a book. It is a tool. A companion. A gentle hand on your shoulder when you are unsure where to begin. It invites families to prepare, not out of fear, but out of love.

If you or someone you care about is entering this season, let this book be your guide. You will find comfort here. You will find clarity. And most of all, you will find hope.

Foreword

This book is not about fear.
It is about clarity.

It was written for families who want to protect dignity, choice, and relationships—before crisis forces decisions to be made under pressure.

Planning for aging, long-term care, and legacy is rarely urgent—until it suddenly is. The Just-In-Case Plan exists to bridge that gap, offering practical guidance, real-world insight, and compassionate honesty about what families face as they age.

This book does not replace professional advice. It empowers readers to engage with professionals more effectively—and to make decisions with eyes wide open.

If it helps you plan earlier, communicate better, or avoid even one preventable mistake, it has served its purpose.

About the Author

Sherri L. Combs is a senior advocate, speaker, and the Founder of **Silver Streak Senior Services**, a trust-first community platform created to help older adults and caregivers navigate aging-related decisions with clarity, dignity, and confidence, before a crisis occurs. After a successful career in private banking, Sherri shifted her focus to advocacy when she saw firsthand how often families were left overwhelmed, misinformed, or unprotected at the most vulnerable moments of their lives.

Sherri has worked directly with seniors, caregivers, physicians, financial institutions, and community organizations across the country. Her approach bridges the gap between legal, financial, medical, and emotional realities, focusing not on theory but on what actually works in the real world. She is known for her ability to explain complex systems in plain language, while preserving humanity, humor, and respect for autonomy.

The Just-In-Case Plan was written to empower families to plan earlier, communicate better, and protect choice—so decisions are made with intention, not pressure.

Acknowledgments

To my family:
Thank you for your patience, your faith in me, and your quiet strength. You have never once complained about the long hours, the constant ideas, the notebooks on every surface, or the moments when this work pulled my attention away. Instead, you stood beside me, encouraged me, and reminded me why this mission matters. Your support has never been conditional, and I do not take that lightly.

To my children & grandchildren:
You have grown up watching me fight for dignity, fairness, and protection for people who are often overlooked. I hope this book shows you that meaningful work is not always easy, but it is always worth doing. You are the reason I believe the future can be better.

And to my husband:
Thank you for standing with me unwaveringly. Through every pivot, every late night, every moment of doubt, you never asked me to shrink my vision or quiet my voice. You believed in this work even when the path wasn't clear, and you believed in me even when I was exhausted. Your steadiness, patience, and love made this book possible

in ways you may never fully see, but I feel them in every page.

This book may carry my name, but it was built with the strength of a family who never once asked me to stop, only to keep going.

With love and gratitude,
Sherri

Introduction

My "Why"

I didn't set out to write this book.

In fact, if I'm being honest, I hoped someone else already had.

I hoped there was a clear, compassionate guide that explained what really happens as we age, how systems actually work, where families get tripped up, and how good people with good intentions still end up overwhelmed, exhausted, and blindsided.

But after years of sitting across desks, kitchen tables, hospital rooms, and quiet waiting areas with families who were doing their very best, I realized something:

Most people don't fail to plan because they don't care. They fail because no one ever showed them how.

I've spent my career at the intersection of money, aging, and family dynamics. I've watched smart, loving families unravel, not because they didn't love each other, but because they didn't know what questions to ask until it was too late. I've seen adult children scrambling under pressure, parents trying to maintain dignity while quietly losing control, and professionals working in silos while families assumed someone else had the full picture.

What struck me most was this:
The crisis almost never came out of nowhere.

There were signs.
There were moments.
There were opportunities to prepare—*just in case*.

But those moments were often brushed aside because the conversation felt uncomfortable, overwhelming, or premature.

And I get that.

Aging isn't a single event. It's a slow shift.
It's the loss of certainty. It's the quiet realization that independence doesn't disappear all at once; it narrows.

For many families, the hardest part isn't the paperwork or the cost.
It's the emotional weight.

The fear of becoming a burden.
The fear of making the wrong decision.
The fear of stepping in too soon, or waiting too long.

This book was written to meet you **before** the crisis.

Not with doom.
Not with pressure.
Not with one-size-fits-all answers.

But with clarity.

I wrote this book because I've seen what happens when families plan early, and what happens when they don't. I've seen how a little preparation can preserve dignity, protect relationships, and dramatically reduce stress for everyone involved. And I've seen how the absence of a plan doesn't prevent hardship; it often guarantees it.

This is not a book about predicting the future.
It's a book about protecting choice.

Choice over where care happens.
Choice over who helps.
Choice over how decisions are made.
Choice over how much chaos your loved ones have to carry on your behalf.

You don't need to do everything at once.
You don't need to be perfect.
You don't need to have all the answers.

You just need a place to start.

This book is that starting point.

If it helps you ask better questions, have more honest conversations, and make even one thoughtful decision before a crisis forces your hand, then it has done exactly what I hoped it would do.

I'm glad you're here.

Let's talk—
just in case.

Dedication

This book is dedicated to Seniors everywhere in every corner of the earth and their caregivers. May you find renewed strength to see your full value and carryon sharing your light with the world.

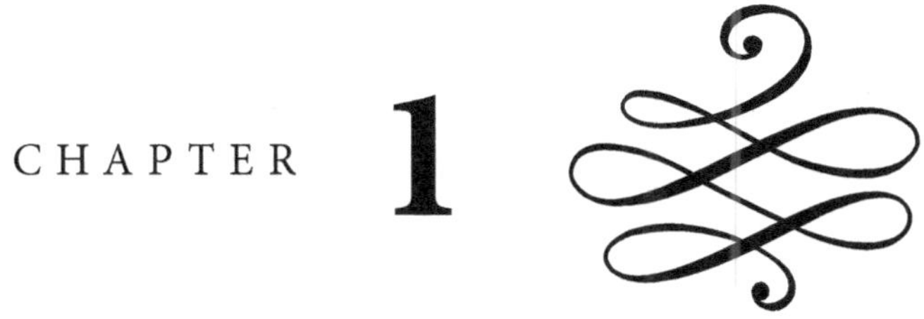

CHAPTER 1

The Illusion of "Later"
A System Under Strain and a Generation at a Crossroads

Most families believe they have time.

Time to talk about aging.
Time to figure things out.
Time to deal with long-term care *later*.

"Later" feels reasonable.
It feels responsible.
It feels calm.

But "later" is quietly becoming the most dangerous assumption we make.

Because while families are waiting, the system is changing underneath them.

We are living longer than any generation before us, and we are doing so inside a care system that was never designed to support this many older adults for this long. Senior living communities are full. Caregivers are scarce. Costs are rising faster than wages. And the demographic wave that experts have warned about for decades has not even fully arrived yet.

This is not a future problem.
This is a now problem.

And the consequences of waiting are no longer theoretical. They show up as rushed decisions, fractured families, financial shock, and care that happens *to* people instead of *with* them.

This chapter is not about fear.
It's about reality.

Because once you understand what is happening at the system level, and why timing matters more than most families realize, "later" stops feeling like a plan… and starts feeling like a risk.

Demographic Turning Points

According to the United States Census Bureau, the year 2030 marks a major demographic turning point for the United States. Beginning that year, every living Baby Boomer, those born between 1946 and 1964, will be age sixty-five or older. For the first time in history, one entire generation will cross into older adulthood at the same moment, shifting the country into a new demographic era.

By 2030, one in every five Americans will be of retirement age. Older adults will make up approximately twenty percent of the population, a proportion the United States has never experienced before. And this shift is only the beginning.

Throughout the 2030s, population growth will slow due to lower birth rates, increased longevity, and the continued aging of the Baby Boom generation. During this decade, immigration rather than natural population increase will become the primary driver of U.S. population growth.

By approximately 2034, older Americans are projected to outnumber children under the age of eighteen for the first time in U.S. history. Census estimates place this shift at roughly seventy-seven million older adults compared with seventy-six and a half million children.

For the first time in history, older Americans will outnumber children.

Although the nation's overall growth is slowing, the total U.S. population is still expected to expand, exceeding four hundred million people by 2058. As this growth continues, the share of Americans over age sixty-five will keep rising through the 2040s and beyond.

The age makeup of our country is changing, and with it, the pressures placed on families, communities, and social systems. By mid-century, there will be significantly fewer working adults supporting significantly more retirees.

The sandwich generation, those caring for children and aging parents at the same time, is growing rapidly.

Employers will need to adapt as more workers between the ages of forty-five and seventy require flexible schedules, remote options, and caregiver support.

When Social Security was created, it was originally designed as a safety net for widows and orphans. During wartime, America temporarily reshaped its workforce to meet extraordinary demands. What was meant to be a short-term accommodation slowly became the norm.

Over time, the country shifted toward an economic model centered on work above all else. Two-week vacations became standard. Sick leave was limited or nonexistent. Long salaried workweeks were expected, not questioned.

Families adapted as best they could. Grandparents often stepped in to help raise children, and many of us grew up as part of the latchkey generation, more independent, but increasingly disconnected from extended family support.

As assisted living and nursing homes became more accessible, many families transferred the responsibility of elder care to institutions. Social Security checks helped offset costs, and society gradually normalized this outsourcing of care.

A generation of children grew up watching this model unfold. Grandparents helped when they could. Later, families relied on facilities when aging parents could no longer live independently.

Was this a moral failure?
Or was it a response to economic pressure that carried an

unintended consequence, a growing human disconnect in how we viewed aging?

Perhaps it was a little of both.

Either way, it was an economic response with real human consequences.

Now, that same generation is aging into the system it helped create. And the demographic shift before us demands something different: a return to intentional, family-centered conversations about aging, care, and planning.

We are standing at the edge of a demographic transformation. The question is not whether it will happen, but whether we will prepare for it or allow it to catch us unprepared.

The Coming Care Crisis

There is another critical piece of this demographic shift that receives far less attention. The United States does not have enough trained medical professionals to care for its rapidly aging population.

According to the American Geriatrics Society and the Association of American Medical Colleges, the country currently has approximately 7,400 certified geriatricians. To meet today's needs, at least 30,000 are required, and projections estimate more than 46,000 will be needed by 2030.

Geriatrics remains one of the lowest-paid medical specialties, despite requiring more time, patience, and complex decision-making. With medical school debt often exceeding two hundred thousand dollars, many young physicians are unable to choose geriatrics, even if they feel called to the work.

The nursing shortage is equally concerning. More than one million nurses are expected to retire by 2030. Many senior living communities already face nursing vacancy rates of twenty to thirty percent. In many cases, nursing homes limit admissions not because of a lack of beds, but because they lack adequate staffing.

A 2009 American Hospital Association report titled *Caring for an Aging America* found that older adults account for forty-four percent of hospital care, thirty-eight percent of emergency medical responses, thirty-five percent of pre-scriptions, and twenty-six percent of physician visits. These percentages have continued to rise as the Baby Boom generation ages.

The care crisis is not coming. It is already here.

The shortage of family caregivers further compounds the problem. AARP reports that the ratio of potential caregivers to older adults will decline from seven to one in 2010, to four to one by 2030, and just two to one by 2050. Families are having fewer children, relocating more frequently, and living farther apart.

Taken together, these trends make one reality unmistakable. The future of caregiving depends on early planning. Families who prepare will be better positioned than those who wait for crisis.

Key Takeaways

- America is aging at a historic pace, with major demographic shifts arriving by 2030.
- There are not enough geriatricians, nurses, or trained caregivers to meet projected demand.
- Family caregiving pools are shrinking, placing increased pressure on fewer people.
- The healthcare system will struggle under the weight of an older population.
- Early planning offers the strongest protection for families.

Important Statistics

- Only 7,400 geriatricians currently practice in the United States, while more than 30,000 are needed today.
- Seniors account for 44 percent of hospital care and 38 percent of emergency medical responses.
- More than one million nurses are expected to retire by 2030.
- Family caregiver ratios are projected to fall to two caregivers for every older adult by 2050.

Sources and Citations

- U.S. Census Bureau. *By 2030, All Baby Boomers Will Be Age 65 or Older.*
- U.S. Census Bureau. *Population Projections: 2020–2060 (P25-1144).*

- U.S. Census Bureau. *Older Americans to Outnumber Children by 2034.*
- American Geriatrics Society. Workforce Data.
- Association of American Medical Colleges. Physician Workforce Reports.
- National Council on Aging. *Older Adults: Key Data Points.*
- AARP. Caregiver Support Ratio Reports.
- American Hospital Association. *Caring for an Aging America* (2009).
- National Council of State Boards of Nursing. Workforce Trends.
- Health Resources and Services Administration. Nursing Projections.

CHAPTER 2

Senior Living Communities
A Candid State of the Union

Senior living communities across the United States are facing a convergence of challenges: rising demand, limited staffing, escalating construction costs, and aging infrastructure. I have attended conferences hosted by some of the largest owners and operators in the senior living space and have spent time with CEOs, property managers, caregivers, and residents themselves. Across the industry, the conclusions are consistent, sobering, and urgent.

In many regions, senior living communities are already operating at high occupancy. Independent living and active adult communities in several markets report occupancy rates between ninety and ninety-six percent. As a result, many operators are reducing their marketing spend because they no longer need it.

When occupancy reaches this level, communities are no longer recruiting residents. They are managing waiting lists. Industry leaders increasingly expect waiting lists to become the standard operating model.

When occupancy exceeds ninety percent, communities stop marketing and start managing waiting lists.

At the same time, new construction is not keeping pace with demand. Developers estimate that building a new senior living community can cost nearly three hundred thousand dollars per unit, depending on location and level of care. Developers estimate that building a new senior living community can cost nearly three hundred thousand dollars per unit, depending on the location and the level of care. Many existing properties require significant rehabilitation, which must be completed while maintaining enough occupancy to avoid displacing current residents.

Rehabilitating an existing community can still cost approximately one hundred fifty thousand dollars per unit. With high interest rates, supply chain constraints, and construction labor shortages, the financial model has become increasingly difficult to sustain.

Passing these costs on to residents is not realistic for most families, nor is it feasible for many government-supported programs.

Staffing shortages further strain the system. Many senior living communities face nursing vacancy rates between twenty and thirty percent. In some cases, nursing homes limit admissions not because beds are unavailable, but because they lack sufficient staff to provide safe care. Compounding the issue, caregiving and nursing roles in senior housing are often among the lowest-paid positions in healthcare, making it difficult to attract and retain workers.

Some communities limit admissions not because they lack beds, but because they lack staff.

In basic economic terms, demand continues to rise, supply remains constrained, and costs are escalating. And the demographic wave driving this demand has not yet reached its peak.

As a result, aging in place will increasingly become the default model for older adults. This shift is not driven solely by preference, but by necessity.

Families who recognize this reality are already planning accordingly. Many are seeking multigenerational homes with dual primary suites, separate living areas, and layouts that allow multiple adults to live together while preserving privacy, dignity, and independence.

Aging in place is no longer a preference. It is becoming a necessity.

Key Takeaways

- Senior living occupancy is already high in many markets, and waiting lists are becoming more common.

- Construction costs and interest rates make rapid expansion of senior housing unlikely.
- Staffing shortages, particularly among nurses, are limiting admissions across the country.
- Aging in place will increasingly become the dominant model of senior care.
- Families who plan ahead for multigenerational living will be better positioned than those who do not.

Statistics Snapshot

- Senior housing occupancy often ranges from the high eighties to the mid nineties in many U.S. markets.
- New senior housing construction averages between two hundred fifty thousand and three hundred fifty thousand dollars per unit, depending on market and care level.
- Rehabilitation costs typically range from one hundred twenty-five thousand to one hundred seventy-five thousand dollars per unit.
- Nursing vacancy rates commonly remain between twenty and thirty percent in senior living communities.

Sources and Citations

- National Investment Center for Seniors Housing and Care (NIC). Senior Housing Occupancy and Construction Data.

- American Health Care Association. Staffing Shortage and Workforce Reports.
- Industry estimates on senior housing construction and rehabilitation costs.
- U.S. Census Bureau. Population and Demographic Projections.

NOTES:

CHAPTER 3

AI in a Supporting Role
How Technology Can Help an Aging Nation

Artificial intelligence will not solve the challenges of an aging society. But used thoughtfully, it can support the people who carry those challenges every day.

One group in particular stands at the center of this conversation: the sandwich generation.

The sandwich generation refers to adults who are simultaneously caring for themselves and their children while also supporting aging parents. These individuals often carry professional responsibilities alongside caregiving duties, navigating competing demands with limited time and energy.

Workplaces do not exist apart from society. They reflect it, shape it, and are shaped by it. Increasingly, both employees and consumers are stepping away from organizations that treat people as expendable rather than human.

There was a time when workers could devote decades to a company and reasonably expect loyalty in return. Pensions and long-term security rewarded commitment. As those systems disappeared, layoffs became commonplace, often driven by shareholder pressure rather than individual performance. The expectation shifted toward constant productivity, emotional compartmentalization, and leaving personal life at the door.

The consequences were predictable. Burnout increased. Work-life balance deteriorated. Many employees stopped seeing themselves as valued contributors and began withholding the very loyalty that had once defined American work culture. Younger generations watched parents lose jobs just before pensions vested, and trust eroded.

Profit is necessary. Profit without humanity is not sustainable.

Traditional top-down command structures no longer function as they once did. Turnover has risen, entrepreneurship has surged, and remote work has reshaped expectations. The pandemic accelerated changes that were already underway, revealing both the benefits and the limitations of digital work.

Profit itself is not the problem. It is essential. But long-term success will belong to organizations that recognize their workforce as a living system, not a disposable machine.

If employers are wise, they will not use AI merely to replace workers and overload those who remain. Instead, they will use it to reduce unnecessary strain and create sustainable, humane work environments.

Used correctly, artificial intelligence can eliminate low-value tasks, streamline routine processes, and return time to people. Time to care. Time to rest. Time to show up for family.

I know many accomplished professionals abroad who work remotely for American companies but refuse to relocate to the United States, even for higher pay. They value protected time off. In many European countries, five weeks of vacation is standard. By comparison, the typical American two-week policy leaves little room for travel, rest, caregiving, or recovery.

Younger generations are pushing back. Millennials and Gen Z are demanding flexibility, mental health support, and realistic workloads. While bundled paid-time-off systems represent progress, they will not be sufficient for an aging workforce that increasingly includes caregivers.

AI can support this transition when used ethically.

AI-driven HR systems can simplify family medical leave requests, caregiver accommodations, and flexible scheduling.
AI can optimize staffing models that support four-day workweeks, hybrid roles, and temporary task redistribution.
AI-enabled employee support platforms can provide mental health tools, eldercare navigation, and resource coordination.

The danger is not AI itself, but using it to reduce people instead of supporting them.

A smaller, more burdened workforce is the opposite of what an aging society needs.

AI Supporting Aging in Place

AI cannot care for aging parents the way a loving child, partner, or friend can. It cannot replace human presence, physical touch, shared history, or the emotional intuition that comes from being known. Caring for an adult who needs supervision is not a technical task it is relational, emotional, and deeply human.

AI cannot offer true empathy, moral judgment, or unconditional love. It cannot fully anticipate complex human risk, interpret subtle emotional cues, or prevent every crisis before it unfolds. It does not eliminate uncertainty, and it does not erase vulnerability.

What AI can do is buy back time—and reduce unnecessary isolation.

When used thoughtfully, AI can ease the administrative burden that quietly exhausts families and caregivers: scheduling, paperwork, documentation, billing, compliance, and routine communication. By removing friction from these tasks, AI creates space for more meaningful human connection instead of competing with it.

In practical terms, AI is already supporting aging in place. Smart home technologies can monitor movement patterns, detect falls, and alert caregivers when something changes. Medication management systems can provide reminders and notify caregivers of missed doses. Health-monitoring tools can track sleep, heart rate, and daily routines, flagging concerning shifts earlier rather than later.

AI can also serve as a *supplemental companion*—not a replacement relationship. It can read aloud to aging eyes, facilitate games and cognitive engagement, offer reminders, provide conversational interaction, and support daily structure. For some older adults, this reduces loneliness between human interactions and helps preserve routine, engagement, and confidence.

Loneliness remains one of the most overlooked public health challenges facing older adults. Health limitations, mobility loss, geography, and driving restrictions can isolate seniors even when families care deeply and are doing their best.

While AI does not have a heart, it does interact with the emotional centers of the human brain. Humans designed these systems, and they reflect human communication patterns. When technology responds with clarity, affirmation, or calm structure, many people experience reassurance, not because the technology cares, but because it supports the human need for connection.

Imagine a senior who is homebound due to health or mobility limitations. Through platforms like Silver Streak Senior Services, isolation does not have to mean abandonment. A trusted AI companion can engage seniors in mentally stimulating activities calibrated to challenge without diminishing ability, gently encourage human connection when withdrawal is detected, provide medication reminders and daily prompts, enable caregiver visibility without invading privacy, and support emergency escalation when concerning patterns appear.

Used wisely, AI extends independence without pretending to replace care. It enhances awareness; it does not eliminate risk. It supports caregivers and older adults by preserving energy for what matters most: real human presence.

Technology should strengthen connection, not substitute it. AI should support caregiving, not replace it.

Key Takeaways

- AI cannot replace human caregiving, emotional support, or presence.
- AI can significantly reduce administrative burdens for caregivers and employees.
- AI tools can support aging in place through monitoring, reminders, and early detection.
- Employers can use AI to create humane, flexible, and sustainable workplaces.
- The future workforce must plan with the expectation that many employees will be caregivers.
- Ethical AI can reduce loneliness and improve the quality of life for older adults.

Statistics Snapshot

- Surveys show older adults are cautiously open to AI for diagnostics and routine support.
- AI fall-detection systems can reduce hospitalizations through early intervention.
- Employers offering caregiver flexibility report higher retention and engagement.
- AI scheduling tools can reduce workload bottlenecks by up to twenty-five percent in some industries.

Sources and Citations

- **AARP**. AI and Caregiving Research.
- OECD and European Union workforce and vacation policy reports.
- HR technology and workplace AI utilization studies.
- Healthcare AI literature on monitoring, fall detection, and medication adherence.
- **Society for Human Resource Management**. AI in HR systems.

Notes

NOTES:

Trusts, Wills, and Beneficiaries
What You Need to Know Before Anything Else

Legal Disclaimer

This chapter is provided for educational and informational purposes only and does not constitute legal, tax, or financial advice. Laws vary by state and change frequently. Readers are strongly encouraged to consult with a licensed attorney, financial advisor, and or tax professional regarding their individual circumstances before taking action.

Great.
Now that the lawyers are happy, let's talk.

Your Family Legacy Begins With You

Most people are not trying to be complicated. They are simply trying to protect what they worked so hard to build.

They want to:

- minimize unnecessary taxes where possible
- avoid probate delays and public exposure
- reduce legal and financial risk
- make sure their wishes actually happen

Think of a will and a trust like shelter from a storm.

A will is like a glass sunroom.
On a calm day, it may be enough. But everything inside is visible to everyone outside. Family. Creditors. Courts. There are no curtains. No privacy.

A trust is like a brick house.
It offers strength, privacy, and protection.

But here is the part many people miss.

You have to actually be inside the house to benefit from it.

If your assets are not properly titled into the trust, the trust offers no protection at all.
Hold onto that image. It matters.

A trust only protects what is inside it.
Paperwork without follow-through is just paper.

A Simple Scenario: Sunny Skies, Light Breeze

No children.
No inherited wealth.
No home ownership.

In a situation like this, you may be fine with:

- properly named beneficiaries on bank accounts
- beneficiaries on retirement accounts and life insurance
- a basic will as a backstop

But even in simple situations, you still need to answer:

- Who makes medical decisions if you cannot?
- Who manages finances during incapacity?
- Who becomes the guardian of a minor or unborn child?

These decisions are handled through medical powers of attorney, financial powers of attorney, and advance directives. These documents work while you are alive.

Do not skip them.

A standard will does nothing while you are living.
A revocable living trust works while you are alive and after death.
Powers of attorney end at death.

And one rule overrides almost everything else.

Beneficiaries override a will.

What a Trust Is and Is Not

A common misconception is that a trust automatically protects assets from creditors or lawsuits.

A standard revocable living trust does not.

In higher net-worth situations, families sometimes use layered planning involving LLCs and coordinated legal structures. That level of planning requires professional guidance and careful execution.

Estate planning is not just paperwork.
It is strategy.

For example, many rental property owners place each property into a separate LLC, then place those LLCs into an irrevocable trust to provide stronger protection options.

Another area people often misunderstand is capital gains on the family home.

When someone purchases a home, the purchase price becomes the starting value for tax purposes. Over time, that home often increases in value. If the home is sold while the owner is still living, capital gains taxes may apply, although many homeowners qualify for significant exclusions on the sale of a primary residence.

At the time of this writing, if you are alive and sell your primary residence, you may qualify for a home sale tax exclusion of up to **$250,000 (single)** or **$500,000 (married)**, provided you have lived in the home for at least **two of the past five years.**

When a homeowner passes away, the rules change. In most cases, heirs receive what is called a **stepped-up cost basis,** meaning the home's value is reset to its fair market value as of the date of death. This typically applies whether the home transfers through a will, probate, or a properly structured trust.

In plain English, this often means heirs may owe little to no capital gains tax if the home is sold shortly after inheritance. Planning tools such as trusts can help streamline the process and avoid probate, but the stepped-up basis itself is **not dependent on having a trust**.

Understanding this distinction can preserve a significant portion of a family's wealth and help prevent unnecessary, fear-based decisions.

That said, laws change. Outcomes vary. Professional guidance matters.

Story 1: The Costly Forgotten Beneficiary

Judy died unexpectedly in her fifties from complications of diabetes.

She had updated her will just three months earlier. She named an executor who had no idea he was named as such until her passing. He was unable and unwilling to take on the role as executor. Her brother stepped up to do the job.

I had advised her to update her beneficiaries as well. She insisted she was covered.

She wasn't.

She never updated an older credit union savings account. One small checking account had a beneficiary, her best friend, who later paid for her cremation. The funds were one thousand dollars short of the cost.

Her car had no transfer-on-death title. Probate would have cost more than the car was worth, so the family allowed the lender to repossess it.

Her family sold everything in the apartment, took time off work, paid extra rent, and barely broke even.

And the largest payout?

Her ex-boyfriend from over fifteen years earlier.

He was the named beneficiary on that savings account. He was not in the will. No one in the family and her current friends even knew his name.

The credit union had no choice.
They cut him a check. He never offered a cent to the family.

The will could not override it.

The law follows beneficiaries, not intentions.

Key Takeaways

- Beneficiaries override wills
- Executors must be willing and informed
- Estate planning attorneys matter, even for small estates

Story 2: The Unfunded Trust

Mrs. Smith arrived at the bank weeks after her husband died, trust documents in hand. Trust documents that contained the will.
Everything looked perfect until I checked the accounts.

My heart sank. My mind raced as I searched for the most compassionate way I could inform her.

He never funded the trust.

Nothing was titled to it.
No beneficiaries were named.
Not the home. Not the accounts. Not the investments.

The bank could not help her. We could not even disclose balances.

Why? She had no legal claim until she went through probate.

Because a trust only protects what is inside it.

Her grief collided with probate, delays, and financial dependence on her children.

A trust you never fund is a promise you never keep.

Key Takeaways

- A trust must be funded
- Paperwork alone does nothing
- Titles and beneficiaries matter

Story 3: When Good Intentions Are Not Enough

Mr. Dale wanted to do the right thing.

After his first wife died, he kept his daughters as beneficiaries. Later, he remarried and added his new wife as a joint owner on his bank account so she could help with expenses.

His will clearly left assets to his daughters, and they were the named beneficiaries on the bank accounts.

Four years later, he died.

Because the account was jointly owned with right of survivorship, the bank released all funds to the surviving joint owner. The account was closed before the daughters even knew. As beneficiaries, they would not have had access until both named owners on the account were deceased.

There was nothing left for the will to control.

Good intentions did not survive bad paperwork.

So what could he have done differently? He could have set up a separate account with the bulk of the inheritance in it, either as a sole owner with his daughters as beneficiaries, or a joint account with just his daughters as co-owners. Or he could have made the checking account with his new wife tenants in common, so at least his half would have gone to his daughters.

It is important to note that an account with his wife and daughters as owners would not have necessarily worked, as it only takes one owner to close an account so anyone of them could have withdrawn funds at any time and closed the account.

It is very important to communicate with your banker about your intentions so they can help you structure your account properly according to the bank's policies.

Adding someone to an account is legally giving them the money.

Key Takeaways

- Joint ownership overrides written intent
- Banks follow titles, not wishes
- A properly structured trust could have prevented this

Chapter 4 – Final Key Takeaways

- Beneficiaries override wills
- A will does nothing during life
- Powers of attorney end at death
- Trusts must be funded to function
- Titles control outcomes
- Good intentions are not enough

NOTES:

CHAPTER 5

Deeds, Probate, Banks, and Real-World Execution

How Plans Succeed or Fall Apart

Chapter 4 focused on what your documents say.
This chapter is more about what actually happens.

This is where good intentions collide with real life.
Banks. Courts. Property titles. Timelines. State laws.
Family dynamics.

This is where plans either work
or quietly unravel.

Story 4: The Cost of Doing It the Hard Way

Two sisters lost their father, a successful New York resident who owned twenty-seven properties. Rental homes. Parcels of land. Even a small strip mall. Which included ownership of a liquor store and a postal center.

By any measure, he had built real wealth.

He believed in simplicity. Everything stayed in his name. He refused trusts and LLCs, convinced they were unnecessary complications. His will was clean, straightforward, and in his mind, more than enough.

It wasn't.

Because he passed away as a New York resident, New York law controlled everything. The sisters could not even open an estate bank account in their home state. Despite using a national bank, they were forced to travel back and forth repeatedly just to complete basic legal and financial steps.

Only the investment accounts with properly named beneficiaries avoided probate. Everything else was trapped.

Years of court involvement followed.
Years of legal fees, appraisals, delays, taxes, and stress.

No privacy.
No shortcuts.

What began as a close sibling relationship slowly eroded under the weight of exhaustion, grief, money, and pressure. By the time the estate was finally settled, the sisters received only a fraction of the estate's original value.

Their father thought he had kept things simple.
What he really did was make everything harder.

Keeping everything "in your name" is not control. It is vulnerability.

Key Takeaways

- Wills do not fully protect complex estates
- Real estate without trusts falls directly into probate
- State residency laws matter deeply
- Probate drains time, money, privacy, and family harmony

Story 5: When Entitlement Rewrites a Legacy

Mr. and Mrs. Henry were married for fifty-two years. Together, they raised three daughters and created what they believed was a fair and loving plan. Everything would go to the surviving spouse, then be divided equally among their children, two daughters from their marriage and one from her previous marriage, whom they had raised together.

When Mrs. Henry passed away, Mr. Henry never probated her will or removed her name from the home's title.

Years later, he came to the bank to refinance the house so he could make safety upgrades and age in place.

The solution should have been simple. An heirship affidavit provided by the title company would suffice. All three daughters would sign, confirming the will and allowing their father to proceed.

Two daughters signed immediately.

One refused.

She demanded to be paid her "share" on the spot. When her father explained that he could not afford to buy her out and that the will had not changed, she forced him into probate to remove his wife's name from the house so he could refinance it.

He tried to reason with her that she would lose because of the provisions in the will.

It cost him thousands of dollars and several months of delay, just to remove his late wife's name from the home.

She received nothing.

And once Mr. Henry saw how quickly trust turned into leverage, he updated his will and disinherited her entirely.

Parents are not required to tolerate financial bullying.

Key Takeaways

- Unprobated wills can block even simple transactions
- Heirship affidavits only work when families cooperate
- Greed and entitlement can permanently rewrite a legacy

Why Deeds Matter More Than People Think

After stories like these, families often ask me,
"How could this have been avoided?"

Sometimes the answer is not a trust.
Sometimes it is a deed.

And sometimes, one properly drafted and recorded document could have saved years of court, thousands of dollars, and immeasurable stress.

Lady Bird Deeds and Transfer on Death Deeds

How Homes Can Transfer Without Court, If Done Right

A Lady Bird deed, also called an Enhanced Life Estate Deed, allows your home to transfer automatically at death while you retain full control during life.

You can sell it.
You can refinance it.
You can change your mind.

Nothing transfers until death.

That distinction matters.

Unlike quitclaim deeds, which transfer ownership immediately and can trigger Medicaid penalties and refinancing problems, Lady Bird and Transfer on Death deeds do not create an immediate gift. In states that recognize them, they often avoid probate and usually avoid the Medicaid five-year lookback rule.

But there is a catch.

These deeds must be properly drafted, properly recorded, and coordinated with the rest of your plan.

Keeping them in a drawer does nothing.
Recording them after death is impossible.

If it is not recorded, it does not exist.

These tools are powerful, but they are not universal. Not every state recognizes them, and they do not automatically protect against Medicaid estate recovery after death.

Used intentionally, they preserve independence and dignity. Used casually, they create chaos.

Story 6: When No One Wants the Job

A grandmother with custody of her grandson tried to do everything right. She created a trust and an LLC. She named her brother as the guardian and a bank as the trustee.

On paper, it looked solid.

In real life, no bank would accept the role. Why? Few banks want to take on the role of trustee unless you are in a Private bank. Which means you have considerable wealth, or liquidity. That definition varies by bank; a national bank may require a minimum of four million, while a smaller regional bank may require one million in liquid assets.

After being turned down by multiple banks, her brother sought to have himself appointed as trustee. The court refused and took over as financial conservator of the estate. Which, according to the trust, would remain in place until this child reached age 30.

What was meant to protect her grandson became a rigid, expensive conservatorship. Every expense required approval. Funds earned minimal returns. The system she feared ended up controlling everything.

Her mistake was not intention.
It was structure.

Courts do not easily release control once involved.

Key Takeaways

- Very few banks serve as trustees
- Naming an institution requires prior confirmation
- Court-supervised conservatorships are costly and restrictive
- Coordination matters more than paperwork

Story 7: "May" vs. "Shall"

A man passed away without a will, leaving modest assets and cooperative heirs. Everyone agreed on how the estate should be divided and hoped to avoid probate.

Under state law, the family *may* use a family settlement agreement as an alternative to formal probate. Their attorney drafted the agreement, and it was properly executed and notarized.

One financial institution accepted it.
Another refused.

Because the word *"may"* is permissive, not mandatory.

The bank that refused required either **Letters Testamentary** or a **Small Estate Affidavit** issued or recognized by the court.

Letters Testamentary are court-issued documents that formally establish who has legal authority to manage and settle an estate. Without them, even a named executor or agreed-upon family representative may be unable to access accounts or transfer assets.

A Small Estate Affidavit is a statutory shortcut available in some states that allows heirs to collect limited assets without full probate—*but only if strict eligibility requirements are met*. Even then, acceptance is not guaranteed.

Financial institutions are not required to honor family settlement agreements or small estate affidavits unless they choose to do so.

The family challenged the bank's decision for years. By the time the dispute ended, the account was nearly classified as abandoned property.

They lost.

The agreement was valid between family members. It could be considered by a court in determining authority, but it did not bind third parties.

One word changed everything.

Key Takeaways

- Legal language matters
- Third parties are not required to accept informal agreements-even when notarized.
- Court documents carry authority that private agreements do not

It is worth noting that a few states such as Texas and California appoint

Chapter 5 – Final Key Takeaways

- Execution matters more than intention
- Courts are expensive and slow
- Banks require authority, not explanation
- Deeds must be recorded to work
- Titles control outcomes
- Family dynamics amplify every flaw

A Final Thought

Titles do not make professionals.
Experience does. Care does. And integrity holds it all together.

Estate planning is not just about documents—it is about people. It requires coordination across law, finance, tax, and lived experience, guided by professionals who understand how systems behave when families are vulnerable.

Your legacy deserves more than completed paperwork. It deserves a plan grounded in experience, built with intention, and carried out by people who care deeply about the humans behind the forms.

CHAPTER 6

How to Start Talking and Keep Talking

Why This Chapter Exists

Every person needs to understand the challenges of aging that face us all in the coming years. Ignoring them will not make them disappear, and it certainly will not make them easier.

I have sat countless times at my desk with families who desperately wanted to talk, but could not find a way in. When I decided to write this book, I knew it was not enough to explain why planning matters. We also need to talk about how to begin and how to continue these conversations with care.

Adult children would come into my office with their parents, hoping to talk about finances, long-term care, or end-of-life wishes, only to watch the conversation shut down before it ever really started. In our culture, autonomy is deeply valued. When these discussions are initiated by someone else, they can feel less like concern and more like a threat to independence, even when that is not the intention at all.

Quite often, parents would ask to speak with me privately. They did not want their children to "know their business." They wanted the conversation contained, controlled, and discreet. And unfortunately, that often meant the discussion never happened at all within the family.

Which raises an important question:
Why could they speak openly with me, but not with the people they loved most?

In many cases, it was not denial.
It was not stubbornness.
It was control.

We tend to vilify that word. Phrases like *"control freak"* and *"micromanager"* reinforce that judgment. Yet self-control is something we admire and expect. Having control over our choices, our bodies, our finances, and how we live our daily lives is fundamental to the freedoms we cherish.

For aging parents, the fear is not necessarily aging itself. It is the realization that decisions may soon be made *for* them instead of *with* them. It is a difficult transition to accept that the children who once questioned our authority may now be viewed as the experts in the family.

And more often than not, that expertise comes full circle.

For adult children, the invitation here is empathy. Pause long enough to imagine how destabilizing that shift can feel. Resistance is often not defiance—it is a final attempt to preserve dignity.

Resistance is often not defiance. It is a bid for dignity.

Over time, I noticed that aging parents tend to fall into two broad categories.

Category One: The Independent, Healthy Fighter

These are the parents determined to embrace their hard-earned wisdom while fighting off the aches, pains, and limitations that come with slowing down. For many, slowing down is not rest. It feels like surrender.

They enjoy being productive. Capable. Independent.

The idea of being reduced to shuttle buses, rocking chairs, and endless cable news is not just unappealing. It is appalling.

They often refuse to discuss how you can help or any sort of plan at all. They do not want to be a burden, not realizing that you not knowing the plan becomes a burden in itself. Being left to guess and hope is stressful at best and terrifying at worst.

They wait until it is too late to ask for help because they fear that once assistance begins, everything will be taken over. Not just the pieces they need help with today, but all of it. However, trying to do it all often leads to devastating consequences that land them exactly where they were trying to avoid.

You are trying to prepare.
They are trying to avoid.

A supportive approach for this category starts with shifting your internal goal. The objective is not to make things easier for you. It is to help your parents age as safely and independently as possible for as long as possible.

Well-intentioned children often slip into parenting their parents. It is not cute. It is not funny. And it quietly breeds resentment and humiliation. These outcomes are almost always unintended, but deeply felt.

Support does not require stripping autonomy. In fact, preserving autonomy is often the most supportive act of all.

Preserving autonomy is often the most supportive act of all.

Category Two: "I'm So Over It. You Take Over."

Some parents are more than ready to hand over responsibility. They are tired. Worn down. And genuinely relieved to let someone else manage the details.
In time, this may happen to all of us.

Still, this shift can place significant emotional and financial strain on families who lack time, resources, or support. It can also accelerate decline because disengagement often leads to faster loss of function.

The temptation here is urgency. Yes, the clock is ticking. But if it is not an emergency, do not treat it like one. That can feel deeply unsettling and trigger shutdown.

A supportive approach for this category is balance.

Rather than you handling everything and your parents handling nothing, collaborate. Decide together what they will continue to manage and what you, or other siblings, will take on.

Shared structure restores dignity and purpose. And remarkably often, it reduces overwhelm on both sides.

You already know which category your parents fall into.

And it is important to recognize this truth.

Silence is where problems begin.

Why Parents Avoid the Conversation

Over and over, I noticed something important.

Men, especially, were far more reluctant than women to talk about long-term care when the conversation did not involve dying. Death felt simpler. One decision. Final.

Aging is different. Aging is a slow unraveling of independence.

It introduces fears we would rather not imagine:

- needing help
- losing autonomy
- someone else choosing meals, medication, or clothing
- and yes, possibly someone changing a diaper

That level of vulnerability is not just uncomfortable. It threatens identity.

Women grow up with a lifetime of medical vulnerability. We are poked, prodded, examined, and told, "Relax, it's routine." Add childbirth, and suddenly half the hospital staff knows your anatomy. We do not love it, but we have had practice facing vulnerability head-on.

Men of this generation, or any generation for that matter, usually see a doctor only when something is falling off, or when their wife finally threatens to drive them there herself. If he has a wife or daughters, statistically, he lives longer. Not because of diet or caution, but because he eventually goes to the doctor just to stop the nagging. (For the record, it is the doctor visit, not the nagging, that extends life.)

Their identity is rooted in being providers, fixers, protectors. They helped build the world we live in. Some in uniform. Others brick by brick.

Women did too. While raising children, holding jobs, serving in the military, and fighting for rights, many younger generations now inherit without realizing the cost.

We stand on the roads they paved.
Our children will stand on ours.

And now we ask these same men and women to imagine vulnerability again.

No wonder responses sometimes sound like:
"If I ever get like that, just push me off a cliff."

Dramatic? Yes.
A solution? No

But buried in humor is fear.

And that fear is exactly why this book exists.

Where "Just In Case" Came From

The title of this book was born from one simple phrase.

I cannot tell you how many times I looked across my desk and said:

"I understand how uncomfortable this is. Tomorrow is not promised. Accidents happen. So just in case, I am not saying this will happen, but just in case it does, how would you want us to prepare?"

That phrase changed everything.

"Just in case" opens doors fear keeps locked.

They could say:
"Well… if that ever happened… this is what I'd want."

The Power of Speaking in Hypotheticals

When people speak in hypotheticals:

- they relax
- they feel less exposed
- they feel less cornered

It doesn't feel like a manifestation
It doesn't feel like surrender or weakness
It feels like a backup plan.

A safety net.

And that small shift opens massive doors.

The Cost of Silence

I have seen what happens when these conversations never occur.

Families fracture. Siblings fight. Guilt, anger, and confusion take over. The difference between families who planned, half-planned, and never planned is profound.

For many families, this conversation is harder than the birds and the bees.

But it is far more important.

Healing the Past to Face the Future

This isn't just a logistical problem.
It's an emotional one.

How do we…

- open the dialogue with our families?
- make real, workable plans?
- prepare ourselves mentally for the role reversal ahead?
- come together—not just as families, but as a nation—to care for our aging population?

And maybe the hardest question of all…

How do we heal the wounds of our childhood enough to care for the people who now need us?

I don't claim to have every answer.
No one does.

But here's what I do know:

It's okay if you're still healing.
It's okay if it's complicated.
It's okay if the emotions are messy.

Your parents weren't perfect.
You aren't perfect.
Your children won't be perfect either.

But in the end, *family is what we have.*
And when life reaches the years where care is required, we either come together or we fall apart.

I have seen adult children so wounded by their past that all they could offer was a check. I understand that child— I have been that child.

I have also seen the opposite: grown children desperate for a confession that will never come—waiting for an 88-year-old parent with cognitive impairment to finally say, *"I was wrong. I hurt you."* That rarely brings resolution. In most cases, the parent believes wholeheartedly that they did their best and cannot grasp why their child is "still upset."

Holding on to resentment while expecting care to go smoothly is like trying to row a boat while holding an anchor. It keeps everyone stuck.

Now, let me be clear—there are situations of severe abuse or neglect so egregious that stepping away is justified and even healthy. No book should guilt you into trauma-bonded obligation. But for the rest—the everyday wounds many of us carry—ask yourself gently:

By refusing to release what hurt me, who am I really punishing now?
Sometimes the person who suffers most is the one gripping the pain.

I've sat with families in every scenario—some laughing together at 90, some fractured into separate rooms because it was the only way forward. Every family is different. But conversations can start, even if they start small.

Conversation Starters That Actually Work

Family dynamics come in all shapes and sizes. That is why no conversation is one size fits all.

Start from the reality of your relationship, not the fantasy version. If you only see family on holidays, dropping the Long-Term-Care Bomb at Thanksgiving may not be your best move. (Unless *they* bring it up, then you have a window.) A little humor may lighten the moment:

"Dad, I promise to try not to crash your wheelchair into the wall at full speed."

Only use this if your family laughs easily and sarcasm is part of the culture. If they're more formal, try a gentler approach:

"Mom, Dad—I'd really like to talk about the future, yours and mine.
Could we set aside some time next week to chat?"

If they avoid the topic or insist *"We've got it handled,"* respond with curiosity, not pressure.

"That's great. Where can I find the instructions if I ever need them?
Would you mind sharing them so I can support your wishes *your* way?"

If they joke about "losing their marbles," play along if humor is safe:

"Perfect, when I'm picking up your marbles, should I store them in a baggie or a cookie tin?"

If humor isn't your style, reassurance works just as well:

"I truly hope you live a long, healthy life and simply drift to sleep in peace, but… just in case… I want to be prepared and honor your wishes."

If there is no plan, or they refuse to share one, hand them this book with love, not pressure. Invite them to go through the checklist in the last chapter:

"If you read this and complete the checklist, I promise you front-row parking for life."
(My personal bribe—feel free to use it.)

Family Dynamics – When *"Just in Case"* Becomes *Just All Wrong*

Hooray! Your parents made a plan. You exhale. Finally, direction, clarity, and paperwork. They hand you the folder, and you suddenly feel like someone just placed a live grenade in your lap. This is the point where many adult children make a critical mistake:

They play ostrich.
Head in the sand.
Paperwork in the junk drawer.
"We'll cross that bridge later…"

Do not do that. If you're handed a plan, your responsibility is to **read it**, understand it, and ask questions FOR CLARITY while everyone is still well enough to give answers.

When You've Been Assigned a Role You Don't Want

Maybe you've been named Executor. Or Medical Power of Attorney. Or the one who's supposed to "pull the plug" and make the life-or-death decisions when the time comes. If you read the instructions and feel your stomach drop, you are not alone. Some roles are **heavy.**

If you truly cannot honor their wishes, you owe your parents honesty *now*, not later in a hospital hallway. If you're an only child, you may have fewer options, but you can still prepare. Counseling, support groups, or planning conversations can help build emotional muscles before the crisis arrives. If extended family exists, an aunt, uncle, or cousin, see whether someone else could be primary, and you serve as backup.

When the *Wrong Person* Gets the Role (in your opinion…)

Now let's flip it. What if your parents assigned an important role to a sibling, and it concerns you? Maybe they're irresponsible. Maybe they avoid conflict. Maybe they can't manage their own finances, let alone someone else's.

This is delicate territory. Questioning their decision can feel like a personal attack, and it is exactly why many parents avoid talking about plans in the first place. Unless there was a cognitive impairment when documents were created, you don't get veto power. From *their* perspective, sharing the plan is a **courtesy.** Challenging it can feel like criticism.

Approach gently. A calm, loving tone matters more than perfect words. You might say:

"I love that you've put so much thought into this. I want to make sure your wishes are carried out smoothly. Can we talk through roles together so we're all confident and prepared?"

Sometimes parents truly do know their children's strengths better than their siblings believe. Other times… they don't. If there are just two of you, change may be difficult. If there are three or more siblings, a united and respectful conversation may help your parents reconsider or at least clarify responsibilities.

The Truth About Siblings

In the best scenarios, siblings rise like a team.
One manages paperwork.
One handles medications and appointments.
One writes checks.
One organizes meals, schedules, and logistics.

Everyone leans into their strengths, and the parents feel supported—not like a burden.

In the worst scenarios, old wounds resurface like ghosts at the table.
Jealousy. Rivals. Old resentments.
Arguments over fairness, inheritance, and responsibility.

Trust fractures. Relationships strain.
The emotional distance becomes wider than the Grand
Canyon.

**No estate plan is strong enough to fix a broken
family dynamic—but a broken family dynamic is
strong enough to destroy even the best plan.**

How to Bring Siblings Together as a United Front

If your parents' plan is in place, the next challenge is often not paperwork—it's **people-work**. Siblings come with
decades of history, inside jokes, rivalries, unspoken hurts,
and childhood labels that seem to stick like glue:

the responsible one
the golden child
the baby
the difficult one
the invisible one

Those roles can resurface fast when aging and care decisions
appear. But here's the good news—**you are all adults now**,
and adults get to choose new roles. Healthy collaboration
begins with one simple mindset shift for everyone involved:

This isn't about who Mom loved more.
This is about honoring their life and wishes.

The goal is not equality of effort, because effort rarely
divides equally.
The goal is **shared respect, teamwork, and clarity.**

Here are a Few Points Outlined to Help Guide You

Step 1: Hold a Sibling Meeting Early

Preferably **before** there's a crisis, before emotions are high, and before decisions feel urgent. This can be in person, on Zoom, or even a group call.

Sample opener:

"We all love Mom and Dad and want to do right by them. Can we talk about how to work together so no one carries the whole load alone?"

Step 2: Identify Strengths (Not Weaknesses)

Not everyone must do everything. In fact, that's where conflict grows. Each sibling is likely better suited to **one lane**:

- One is organized and good with forms → *paperwork manager*
- One lives nearby → *appointments, errands, check-ins*
- One is financially stable → *contributes money*
- One brings joy, patience, or humor → *emotional support*
- One is tech-savvy → *medical portals, online communication*

This is how **everyone contributes without comparison or resentment.**

Step 3: Put Responsibilities in Writing

Not to be formal or cold, but to be **clear**. A simple shared document or group text summary prevents misunderstandings later.

"Sarah will handle medical scheduling.
Mike will manage finances and bills.
Jen will organize groceries, rides, and meals."

Clarity saves relationships. Ambiguity ruins them.

Step 4: Communicate Regularly

Short updates prevent suspicion and confusion.

- A weekly group text recap
- Shared notes via Google Drive
- A 15-minute Sunday check-in

Remember, silence invites assumptions.
Assumptions breed resentment.
Communication preserves trust.

Step 5: Leave Room for Real Life

Jobs, little kids, health issues, these things vary between siblings. Someone may carry more weight at one phase, and another may pick up later. Try to release the scoreboard mentality.

The measure of fairness is not sameness, it's willingness.

If everyone helps in a way that fits their season of life, no one burns out, and everyone feels valued.

Step 6: Revisit the Plan as Life Changes

Care needs shift. Finances shift. A sibling may move or fall ill. Revisit roles without guilt or judgment as a family evolves.

Caring for aging parents is not a sprint—it's a marathon with hills, setbacks, and water stations along the way.

The Goal Is Simple

Not perfection.
Not identical effort.
Not approval from your siblings or parents.

The goal is honoring your parents with dignity, without destroying sibling relationships in the process.

1. Scripts & Strategies for Difficult Siblings

(The bossy one, the absent one, the financially unstable one... we all know them)

Every family has at least one sibling who complicates the process. Maybe they are the *bossy general* who wants control of everything. Maybe they avoid involvement, disappear during the hard moments, or resurface only to criticize decisions others made. Others may be financially unstable, emotionally reactive, or struggle to handle paperwork or medical discussions. The key is recognizing patterns early and setting boundaries before resentment grows. A calm, direct conversation can reset expectations:

"We all want what's best for Mom. Let's divide roles based on strengths so no one feels overwhelmed or shut out."

If communication becomes tense or circular, a neutral third party can help. **Family mediators, elder care counselors, or social workers** can guide structured conversations and help navigate disagreements. Mediation can be incredibly valuable—but it is also important to acknowledge it can be **costly** and not always accessible. Use it when stakes are high, decisions are time-sensitive, or emotions are blocking progress. Further along in this chapter, I expounded on this resource in a section titled "third basemen".

2. Signs One Sibling Is Carrying Too Much (and How to Address It)

Often, caregiving quietly falls onto the shoulders of the most capable or nearest sibling. At first, they may handle appointments, bills, house repairs, and late-night emergencies with grace… until exhaustion creeps in. Burnout rarely announces itself—it shows up as irritability, withdrawal, guilt, physical fatigue, or outbursts that seem "out of character." Pay attention when one sibling carries the emotional or logistical weight while others unintentionally drift into the comfortable role of spectator.

Caregiving is not meant to be a **solo endurance event**. When one sibling is drowning, everyone eventually pays the price—relationships strain, resentment grows, and parents suffer from inconsistency. If you notice the load is uneven, bring it up gently:

"You're doing a lot. How can we better support you? What can we take off your plate?"

If agreements break down or one sibling refuses to contribute, this is where **mediation or facilitated family meetings** may help redistribute responsibilities fairly. Again—professional mediators can be extremely effective, but sessions can add up financially, so use them strategically when communication alone no longer works.

3. When Siblings Will Not Work Together

Some families simply cannot collaborate. Old wounds, personality conflicts, estranged relationships, or financial disagreements can make unified caregiving nearly impossible. In these cases, structure becomes your savior. Keep communication factual, short, and documented. Use email or written notes rather than emotional phone calls. Define roles clearly, set boundaries, and avoid trying to force emotional connection during a practical season of care. You cannot heal 30 years of conflict while also managing medications, mobility aids, and doctor appointments.

When conflict stalls progress, **a professional mediator, eldercare attorney, or neutral third party** can step in to create agreements and protect decisions. This can reduce emotional friction but comes with a financial cost. Sometimes the best solution is dividing responsibilities rather than forcing teamwork. Not every family becomes a Hallmark movie, and that's okay. The goal is safe, dignified care—not perfection.

4. When You Are the Only Child

Being an only child can feel like both a privilege and a heavy burden. You don't have to negotiate or argue with siblings—but you also don't have help dividing tasks, decisions, and emotional labor. If you are the sole caregiver, preparation becomes your greatest tool. Build a support team early—neighbors, extended relatives, church friends, community groups, or paid care services. No one said *you* must be every role: nurse, chauffeur, accountant, therapist, maid, advocate, and personal cheerleader. You will need rest too.

Therapists, senior-care advisors, and **family mediators (if extended relatives are involved)** can support decision-making, though this route can be costly. Many single caregivers find strength in local support groups, online forums, or respite programs. Remember: asking for help is not a weakness—it is wisdom. Your parents would not want your health to fail in order to extend theirs.

Resources for Families Navigating Long-Term Care & Difficult Conversations

Because having support matters — and no one should walk this road alone.

Silver Streak Support & Services

Silver Streak Senior Services — Online Directory A growing, user-friendly search platform designed to help seniors and families quickly locate **local, vetted service providers**, resources, and community support. This directory includes businesses that have undergone background, license, and insurance verification, so families can connect with trusted professionals more confidently. You'll also find links to many of the national and community resources listed below — all in one place. Website: https://SilverStreakSeniorServices.com

Silver Streak Senior Solutions — Public Charity A non-profit branch created to support seniors who may be struggling financially. In certain situations, **financial assistance may be available** for home repairs, mobility needs, safety upgrades, respite relief, or other essential aging-in-place support. Funding is based on need, availability, and board approval. Website: *SilverStreakSeniorSolutions.org*

(These two sister-organizations work hand-in-hand — one connecting seniors to trusted help, the other lifting those who may not be able to afford it.)

Free & Low-Cost Community Resources

Area Agency on Aging (AAA)
Local branches offer support with benefits counseling, Medicare questions, caregiver planning, and education. Search: *"Area Agency on Aging + your county/state"*

Senior Centers & Community Programs
Often provide support groups, legal clinics, social workers, and wellness checks.

Meals on Wheels
More than meal delivery — often includes safety visits and case management referrals.

AARP Caregiver Resources
Guides, workshops, and online tools for family planning. aarp.org/caregiving

Caregiver Support & Education

Family Caregiver Alliance — caregiver.org
Alzheimer's Association — alz.org / 24-hr Helpline:
1-800-272-3900
Eldercare Locator — eldercare.acl.gov

Support groups, education, planning guides, and help understanding care options.

Professional Help (When a Neutral Guide is Needed)

Elder Law Attorneys — estate planning & future care decisions
Geriatric Care Managers — coordinate appointments & care plans
Family Therapists — support emotional healing & role reversal
Family Mediators — facilitate difficult conversations

Mediation can be extremely helpful when siblings disagree or decision-making stalls — but it can also be costly, so consider this option when communication alone isn't enough.

Technology & Tools to Coordinate Care

- Shared Google Drive or Dropbox folder
- Weekly family Zoom or group text thread
- Apps: CaringBridge, Lotsa Helping Hands, Medisafe, Abridge

Technology lightens the mental load and keeps everyone informed.

Practical Steps You Can Take Today

✔ Talk early — clarity is a gift to your future self
✔ Keep important documents accessible to more than one person
✔ Assign roles based on strengths, not birth order
✔ Check in regularly & share updates transparently
✔ Ask for help before burnout becomes resentment
✔ Remember — care is not meant to be carried alone

You Are Not Alone in This

Long-term care requires heart, patience, and support. You deserve resources that make this journey more manageable, hopeful, and human. Whether through Silver Streak, national organizations, or community programs, help exists — and every step you take toward planning now protects peace later.

Too many families believe they are failing when they feel overwhelmed. They are not. The system is complex, fragmented, and often difficult to navigate even for professionals. Feeling unsure does not mean you are unprepared — it means you are human.

Planning does not remove uncertainty, but it does remove isolation. When families understand their options, identify support, and communicate openly, they move from fear to footing. This book was written to remind you that you do not have to do everything at once, you do not have to do it perfectly, and you do not have to do it alone.

Sometimes You Need a "Third Baseman"

Sometimes the most effective voice in a family conversation is not the adult child.

It is the third baseman.

A third baseman is a trusted outside voice. A family friend. A respected professional. A senior advocate. A well-liked relative. Someone without emotional baggage or a hidden agenda.

They are not there to take over.
They are there to reassure.

They help parents hear:
"Yes, your kids are thinking clearly."
"Yes, this decision makes sense."
"Yes, it may be time."

I have been the third baseman professionally and personally.

Recently, my ex-father-in-law, Tom, was telling me about his medical issues. He lives with my kids. They hide his keys. They are terrified of his driving.

Tom is retired military and has put more miles on his motorcycle across this nation than anyone I know. To him, driving is independence.

I listened. I showed concern. I did not interrupt.

Then I said, gently, "You know, Tom, if that is what is going on, it is time to give up your car keys. And that really sucks. I'm sorry."

He looked at me and said, "Yeah, it does."

I said, "It's coming for all of us sooner or later. Now you get to be the backseat driver. Which grandkid are we nicknaming James? Haven't you always wanted to say 'Home, James' to someone else?"

We both laughed.

The family exhaled.

Peace was preserved.

It was a small victory out loud and a quiet, painful loss of independence inside. That grief deserves space and grace.

Sometimes the message is right. It just needs the right messenger.

I reminded the kids that he is now grieving a major loss of independence over something he loved doing. How would you feel? Allow him space and grace for a while as he adjusts to this new reality.

What a Good Third Baseman Looks Like

A good third baseman:

- is trusted by your parents
- has no stake in inheritance
- brings calm, not control
- supports family decisions without replacing them
- respects boundaries

If your parents trust someone like this, do not compete with that voice.

Leverage it.

Third Baseman Checklist: Choosing the Right Senior Advocate or Trusted Voice

This checklist can help families identify whether someone is a good fit for this role.

Who Might Serve as a Third Baseman

- A well-liked extended family member
- A longtime family friend
- A trusted professional such as:
  - banker
  - attorney
  - financial advisor
  - realtor
  - senior advocate or care navigator

A faith leader or community elder

Paid or unpaid roles can work. What matters most is **trust and boundaries**.

Essential Qualities to Look For

- Trusted by your parent, not just by you
- Calm, respectful, and patient
- Comfortable discussing difficult topics without pressure

- Able to reinforce decisions without taking control
- Willing to defer final authority to the family
- Not emotionally reactive or divisive
- Understands aging, independence, and dignity

Critical Boundaries (Non-Negotiable)

- No role in inheritance or estate distribution
- No financial control unless formally and legally assigned
- No pressure to be added to wills, trusts, or accounts
- Transparency with the family when appropriate
- Willingness to step back if asked

The best third basemen support decisions. They do not benefit from them.

About Compensation and Gifts

An advocate helps families navigate some of the most treacherous territory imaginable; they become like part of the family. A voice of reason, peace, and a path forward. No wonder you want to include them in family celebrations. This is a perfectly normal response.

This is where families often feel unsure, so clarity matters.

- Paid professionals should be compensated through **clear, documented agreements**
- Unpaid advocates may receive **small, appropriate tokens of appreciation**
- Gifts should never influence decisions or access

- Compensation should never reduce funds needed for care
- When in doubt, keep it simple and modest

Appropriate appreciation often looks like:

- a meal
- flowers
- a handwritten note
- a small gift tied to a holiday or milestone
- a trip to the spa

What matters is **intent and proportion**, not price.

Red Flags to Watch For

- Requests to be added to financial accounts or documents
- Pressure to be named in estate plans
- Discouraging family communication
- Creating secrecy around decisions
- Speaking *for* parents instead of *with* them
- Resistance to professional oversight

If something feels off, pause. Trust your instincts.

How to Introduce the Third Baseman Role

A simple, respectful way to frame it:

"Mom, you seem comfortable talking with them. Would you be open to having them help us think through a few things together so we're all on the same page?"

This keeps autonomy intact while expanding support.

Why This Works

A third baseman does not replace family.

They **support family**.

They help parents feel respected instead of managed. They help children feel reassured instead of adversarial. They turn tension into teamwork.

And when done well, they protect the very thing everyone wants to preserve.

Peace.

NOTES:

____

____

____

____

____

____

____

CHAPTER 7

The Realities of Long-Term Care
What It Is, What It Isn't, and Why Families Get Blindsided

Why This Chapter Exists

Most families do not avoid long-term care planning because they don't care.

They avoid it because the system is confusing, the language feels intimidating, and the price tags seem unreal… right up until the moment it becomes painfully personal.

Long-term care planning is not about expecting the worst. It is about protecting choice.

Choice over:

- where care happens
- who provides it
- how decisions are made
- and whether a family stays financially intact while doing the right thing

This chapter exists to bring clarity to a topic that is almost always discussed too late and almost always during crisis.

Insurance companies underestimated the cost of long-term care decades ago. Now they are paying for it.
That cost is now being passed on to families through rising prices, stricter underwriting, and longer exclusion lists.

1. What Long-Term Care Really Means (and What Actually Triggers It)

Long-term care is not defined by a building.It is defined by **need**.

Long-term care includes medical and non-medical support for people with chronic illness, disability, or functional decline. Much of it involves help with everyday tasks known as **Activities of Daily Living**, or ADLs.

The six commonly recognized ADLs are:

- Bathing
- Dressing
- Toileting
- Transferring (getting in and out of bed or a chair)
- Continence
- Eating

A common trigger for long-term care services and many insurance policies is the inability to perform **two or more ADLs without assistance,** or the presence of a qualifying cognitive impairment.

That detail matters.

Families often assume long-term care begins with a diagnosis. In reality, it usually begins with a **function problem**:

- "Mom can't safely bathe alone anymore."
- "Dad is falling."
- "She's skipping meals."
- "He can't manage the bathroom at night."

Long-term care begins where independence ends.
Sometimes gradually.
Sometimes overnight.

2. The Levels of Care (and Why Costs Rise So Fast)

Long-term care exists on a continuum.
As care becomes more hands-on, more specialized, and more supervised, costs rise quickly.

In-Home Support

Many families want care to remain at home as long as possible. In-home support can include:

- Companion care and supervision
- Help with personal care such as bathing, dressing, and mobility
- Meal preparation, transportation, and routine assistance

Some home services are medical. Many are not.
That distinction matters because **Medicare and**

traditional health insurance generally do not pay for ongoing custodial care.

Community and Facility-Based Care

As needs increase, families often explore:

- Assisted living
- Memory care
- Skilled nursing facilities

Here's the part families don't feel until they are already on the slope:

Costs do not rise in a straight line.
They rise in **leaps** tied to safety risk, nighttime needs, mobility loss, or cognitive decline.

3. Three Different Definitions That Change Everything

One reason families feel lost is because the definition of "long-term care" changes depending on who you're talking to.

Social Security

Social Security is income support.
It helps pay bills. It does **not** function as a long-term care benefit.

Social Security is income support.
It helps pay basic living expenses such as housing, utilities, and food.

It is **not** a long-term care benefit and was never designed to fund caregiving services.

Medicare

Medicare is health insurance.
It is excellent at many things.

But Medicare itself is very clear:
It generally does **not** pay for long-term custodial care, whether at home or in a facility.

Where families get confused is that Medicare *does* pay for things that sound similar, and they will often refer to it as long-term care, such as:

- Hospice care
- Short-term skilled nursing facility care under very specific conditions

Those are not the same as long-term custodial care.

Hospice focuses on comfort at end of life.
Long-term care focuses on daily living and ongoing support.

Insurance Companies

Insurance policies speak contract language, not family language.

Policies define:

- What qualifies as an ADL limitation
- How many ADLs trigger benefits

- Who must provide care
- What documentation is required

This is where many families discover a painful truth: **Coverage is not the same as access.**

4. Can Family Members Be Paid to Provide Care?

This question comes up constantly:
"If I'm doing the work, why can't the system pay me?"

Here's the plain-English answer:

- Social Security does not pay family caregivers
- Medicare generally does not pay for custodial care-giving by family
- Long-term care insurance depends on the policy and often requires licensed caregivers
- Medicaid sometimes allows paid family caregiving under specific state programs

The takeaway:
This is usually a **state-specific Medicaid question**, not a Medicare or Social Security one.

5. Medicaid: When It Kicks In and Why It Feels So Complicated

Medicaid is often the program families assume Medicare will be.

Medicaid **can** pay for long-term care.
But only for people who meet both medical and financial eligibility rules, which vary by state.

Medicaid is federally structured but state administered. That means advice that works in one state can be dangerously wrong in another.

What Medicaid Often Covers

- Nursing facility care
- Certain home and community-based services (varies by state)

Countable vs. Non-Countable Assets

Medicaid divides assets into categories.

Often countable:

- Cash and savings
- Investment accounts
- Additional property

Often excluded (with conditions):

- Personal belongings
- One primary residence in many cases
- One vehicle
- Certain prepaid burial arrangements

Here is what families often learn too late:
Even if a home is excluded during life, **estate recovery may apply after death**, depending on state rules.

The Look-Back Rule: Why Last-Minute Fixes Backfire

Medicaid has transfer rules designed to prevent people from giving away assets simply to qualify.

The look-back period examines financial transfers made prior to application.

Last-minute money moves often cause:

- Delays
- Penalty periods
- Temporary ineligibility

Planning works best **before crisis**, not during it.

6. When One Spouse Needs Care and the Other Is Still at Home

This is one of the hardest realities families face.

Federal Medicaid law includes **spousal impoverishment protections** so the spouse at home is not financially destroyed simply because their partner needs care.

In plain English:

- Assets are reviewed together
- A protected portion may remain with the community spouse
- In some cases, income can be allocated to support the spouse at home

Families often fear losing the house.
In many cases, the home is not immediately forced to be sold if a spouse remains living there, though estate recovery may still be a future consideration.

This is one of the rare places where the system openly acknowledges reality:
A long-term care crisis can financially destroy the healthy spouse without safeguards.

Medicaid in Plain English

Medicaid is the primary public program that pays for long-term care when eligibility requirements are met.

It is:

- Needs-based
- State-specific
- Complex by design

It is not Medicare.
It is not automatic.
And it should never be approached casually.

An Ethical Pause Worth Taking

Many families are advised to "hide assets" to qualify for Medicaid.

It is worth stopping here.

Medicaid exists to protect people with limited means. When families with significant resources intentionally shift care costs to taxpayers so inheritances remain intact, a harder question emerges:

Is that fair?

Planning is not just about protecting money.
It is about responsibility, dignity, and the kind of care we would want if cost were not the driving factor.

7. The Insurance Angle: Rules, Triggers, and the Cost Gap

Long-term care insurance exists because Medicare does not cover custodial care.

But insurance introduces its own realities:

- Benefit triggers
- Elimination periods
- Documentation requirements
- Licensed caregiver rules

Families are often shocked by how formal care must become before benefits start.

And then there is the gap:
A policy may say "$400 per day."

What happens when care costs $800?

Or when beds are scarce?

Insurance is a tool.
It is not a guarantee.

8. Placement Agencies: Why Some Families Feel Burned

Many families reach out for placement help and feel overwhelmed by sales calls, poor matches, and impersonal processes.

That experience is real.

But it is not universal.

There are smaller, boutique care advocates who explain options, curate choices, and treat families like people instead of transactions. Many of those professionals can be found through Silver Streak Senior Services, where the goal is clarity, not chaos.

Closing: The Most Honest Thing I Can Tell You

Planning is not just about what you do.
It is about **when** you do it.

Waiting until your late eighties or nineties often means:

- Doctors are chosen for you
- Living arrangements are decided in crisis
- Independence narrows quickly

Planning earlier preserves:

- Choice
- Community
- Relationships
- Dignity

Avoiding the conversation does not prevent the outcome. Avoiding the plan often **creates the crisis**.

If you take only one thing from this chapter, let it be this:

Good planning is not about predicting the future. It is about protecting dignity, choice, and the people you love **before the system makes those choices for you**.

NOTES:

____

____

____

____

____

____

____

____

CHAPTER 8

Self-Insuring for Long-Term Care
What It Really Means

Important Disclaimer

This chapter is provided for educational purposes only and is not intended as financial, legal, tax, or insurance advice. Long-term care costs, insurance products, tax rules, and public benefits vary by state and change frequently. Always consult qualified professionals before making decisions related to long-term care planning.

Before We Talk Strategy, We Need the Truth

Most people don't avoid long-term care planning because they're irresponsible.
They avoid it because the subject feels heavy… and the math feels rude.

But there are three facts worth your full attention:

1. A large percentage of people over age 65 will need some form of long-term care.

2. In a married couple, the odds are high that **at least one spouse** will need care.
3. Hoping to be the exception is not a strategy.

A healthy lifestyle is wonderful.
Good genetics are helpful.
Positive thinking is lovely.

But none of those come with a warranty.

Another dangerous assumption I hear constantly is this:

"We'll just take care of each other."

It sounds loving.
It sounds loyal.
It can also be an extraordinary burden to place on someone you love.

By the time long-term care is typically needed—often in the late 70s or 80s—your spouse is likely dealing with their own limitations. Dementia, Parkinson's, stroke recovery, mobility loss, and chronic illness often overlap in couples.

Caregiving is physically demanding work:

- transfers in and out of bed
- bathing and personal hygiene
- incontinence care
- dressing
- meal prep and feeding
- medication management
- transportation
- all while sleep-deprived and emotionally exhausted

Young, healthy people find this taxing.
Asking an elderly spouse to shoulder it can be unrealistic, and sometimes impossible.

A Reality I've Seen Repeatedly

I once knew a group of seniors who made a heartfelt pact: They would take care of one another so their children wouldn't have to.

It was a beautiful idea.
It was also unworkable.

One by one, friends became unable to help due to illness, injury, or their own need for care. Eventually, the healthiest among them—the last one standing—had to move closer to medical support and family.

Plans rooted in optimism but not reality tend to collapse right when they're needed most.

What "Self-Insuring" Actually Means

Self-insuring does **not** mean ignoring risk.
It means choosing **control** over the transfer of risk

When someone self-insures for long-term care, they intentionally plan to pay for future care using some combination of:

- investment assets
- home equity
- income streams (Social Security, pensions)

- cash-value life insurance
- annuities with long-term care features
- or a coordinated mix of the above

This approach is **intentional—not accidental**.
And it requires honest math.

The First Thing You Must Understand About Money

As wealth advisor **Karen Stawicki** teaches in *The Power of 3*, money can only do **one of three jobs** at any given time:

- It can grow
- It can stay liquid
- It can create income

It cannot do all three at the same time.

Asking money to be an emergency fund, grow aggressively, and provide monthly income isn't financial planning — it's financial fantasy.

This framework is deceptively simple, yet profoundly clarifying. When each dollar is assigned a clear role, decisions become simpler — even when they aren't easy.

You cannot ask money to:

- be an emergency fund
- grow aggressively
- and provide monthly income

Self-insuring starts with accepting this reality. Once you do, the decisions become clearer — even when they aren't comfortable.

I highly recommend *The Power of 3*, co-authored by Karen Stawicki and her daughter and business partner, **Samantha Irish**, for deeper insight into this approach and other practical wealth strategies. After years of sitting with families in financial advisory offices, I've found that the truly good advisors — the ethical, thoughtful ones — are aligned with these principles. It is well worth the read.

When Long-Term Care Is Typically Needed

Most long-term care is needed later in life, but not always.

Many families plan using a conservative **five-year window**, not because everyone needs five years, but because enough people do that it's prudent.

What matters most is not guessing the timeline.
It's making sure **flexibility exists when timing stops being polite**.

Insurance vs. Self-Insuring: The Real Trade-Off

Insurance is not about winning.
It's about **risk transfer**.

Self-insuring is not about being cheap.
It's about **control**.

Traditional long-term care insurance can offer leverage—*if* you qualify and *if* you keep it.

Self-insuring offers flexibility—*if* you have assets and structure.

The question is not:

"Which is best?"

The question is:

"Which trade-offs can your family live with?"

A Simple Reality Check

A portfolio can look strong on paper until long-term care enters the picture.

Care costs can turn *"we're fine"* into *"we need a plan"* very quickly—especially once you factor in:

- inflation
- taxes
- market timing
- and the needs of a surviving spouse

This is where many families realize too late that **not all dollars are equal**, and not all assets are easy to use under pressure.

Why Flexibility Matters More Than Optimization

One of the most overlooked risks in long-term care planning is **rigidity**.

Care rarely arrives:

- on schedule
- during good market years
- when paperwork is neat
- or when everyone agrees

Self-insuring, when done intentionally, allows families to:

- pay for care at home or in a facility
- modify a home instead of moving
- hire caregivers directly
- adapt when availability of care is an issue

Flexibility doesn't mean chaos.
It means **options**. And options are dignity.

Is It Ever "Too Late" to Self-Insure?

People often ask:

"I'm already 70… is it too late?"

In many cases, the answer is **no**.

Traditional long-term care insurance becomes harder—
or impossible—to obtain as health changes. Self-insured
strategies often have:

- no underwriting
- no health questionnaires
- no age limits

You already own the assets.
You already control how they're used.

The Honest Bottom Line

Self-insuring isn't about being fearless.
It's about being honest.

Honest about the odds.
Honest about the costs.
Honest about what your spouse can realistically carry.
Honest about what you want your children to experience.

The goal is not to reject professionals.
The goal is to understand enough to ask better
questions—and to build a plan that protects dignity and
choice **before** you need it.

Closing Thought

Good planning isn't about predicting the future.
It's about preparing for reality.

And reality has a way of arriving whether we're ready or
not.

Self-insuring, done thoughtfully, is not avoidance.
It is stewardship.

CHAPTER 9

Advanced Strategies for Funding Long-Term Care
When Flexibility Matters More Than Labels

Important Disclaimer

This chapter is provided for educational purposes only and is not intended as financial, legal, tax, or insurance advice. Products, tax rules, benefits, and eligibility requirements vary by state and change over time. Always consult qualified professionals before implementing any strategy discussed in this chapter.

Why This Chapter Exists

By now, one thing should be clear:

There is no single "right" way to plan for long-term care.

There are only **informed trade-offs**.

This chapter exists for families who:

- want more flexibility than traditional insurance provides
- may be past the age or health window for certain policies
- want to protect a surviving spouse
- understand that availability—not preference—often drives care decisions
- want options that still work when plans change

These are **advanced tools**, not magic solutions.
Used thoughtfully, they can expand choice.
Used blindly, they can create confusion.

The goal here is understanding—not persuasion.

A Critical Reframe Before We Begin

Advanced planning is not about chasing the "best" product.

It's about answering better questions, such as:

- *What happens if care is needed longer than expected?*
- *What if no community living bed is available?*
- *What if care must happen at home?*
- *What if markets are down?*
- *What if my spouse is still living and needs stability?*

Flexibility is not a luxury in long-term care planning.
It is a requirement.

Annuities: Without the Baggage

If you grew up hearing, *"Never buy an annuity,"* you're not alone.

Historically, that reputation was often earned.

Earlier generations of annuities were:

- poorly explained
- expensive
- inflexible
- misused
- and sometimes sold where they did not belong

But the annuity market has changed dramatically.

Today, **certain annuities—used intentionally—can play a meaningful role in long-term care planning**.

They are not for everyone.
But they are worth understanding.

Annuities With Long-Term Care Riders

Some modern annuities include **long-term care riders** that increase the value of the annuity if care is needed.

Here's the key distinction families often miss:

These products are not designed to trap your money. They are designed to **preserve access while adding leverage if care occurs.**

How It Works (Plain English)

- You place money into an annuity (often a lump sum)
- The annuity grows according to its contract
- If long-term care is needed and medically certified, the rider:
    o increases the amount available for care
    o often multiplies the interest earned
- If long-term care is **never used**, many of these annuities:
    o return unused principal
    o or provide a death benefit to heirs

This directly addresses the "what if I never need care?" concern that causes many families to reject traditional long-term care insurance.

Unused Benefits: A Quiet but Important Evolution

One of the most significant changes in today's annuity landscape is this:

There are now annuities that:

- provide enhanced benefits **if** long-term care is needed
- **and** return excess principal if care is never required

This means the money:

- remains yours
- can be redirected

- can support a spouse
- can pass to heirs

That alone has shifted the conversation for many families.

Why Flexibility Matters More Than Facility Access

Here is a reality families often don't plan for:

Sometimes, **there is no availability** in assisted living or memory care.

Beds can be scarce.
Staffing shortages are real.
Waitlists are common.

In those moments, the question is not:

"What did we plan for?"

It becomes:

"What can we do right now?"

Annuities with LTC riders may allow funds to be used for:

- in-home care
- paying caregivers directly
- supplementing family caregiving
- bridging gaps while waiting for placement

That flexibility can be the difference between panic and control.

Surrender Schedules: The Part Everyone Fears

Most annuities include a **surrender schedule**, often lasting around 7–10 years.

This simply means:

- if you cancel early for non-qualifying reasons, a declining penalty applies

What is often overlooked:
Most annuities **waive surrender charges** for:

- long-term care
- terminal illness
- critical illness
- death

The purpose is not to lock you in.
It is to discourage short-term use of a long-term tool—
while still allowing access when life happens.

Where Annuities Fit—and Where They Don't

Annuities are best viewed as:

- **preservation tools**
- **liquidity stabilizers**
- **long-term care enhancers**

They are not designed to:

- outperform aggressive investments
- replace all retirement planning
- be used impulsively

Clarity of purpose matters.

IRS Code Section 213: A Strategy Few People Know

Now let's talk about something rarely discussed—but incredibly important **when care is actually happening**.

The Basic Concept

Money in traditional IRAs and 401(k)s has not yet been taxed. Ordinarily, every dollar withdrawn is taxable income.

However:

IRS Code Section 213 allows taxpayers to deduct unreimbursed medical expenses that exceed **7.5% of adjusted gross income (AGI)**.

Qualifying long-term care expenses **count** as deductible medical expenses.

Why This Matters During Long-Term Care

When someone requires long-term care:

- expenses are often $8,000–$15,000 per month
- those costs can dramatically offset taxable income

This creates a planning opportunity:

Instead of preserving pre-tax retirement accounts at all costs, families may intentionally use them **for care**, while preserving after-tax assets for:

- a surviving spouse
- housing stability
- future flexibility

A Simplified Example

Imagine:

- You withdraw $200,000 from a traditional IRA in a year
- Your qualifying long-term care expenses total $200,000
- 7.5% of AGI equals $15,000

Result:

- $185,000 may be deductible
- Only ~$15,000 remains taxable

This is **not a loophole**.
It is existing tax law—used at the right time, with the right coordination.

This is not a DIY strategy.
It requires professional guidance.

But when used correctly, it can be powerful.

Why This Strategy Often Preserves the Surviving Spouse

Many families instinctively spend:

- cash
- brokerage accounts
- home equity

…first.

But those assets are often the most flexible for a surviving spouse.

Using pre-tax retirement dollars **during care**, when deductions are available, can preserve:

- after-tax assets
- housing
- long-term income flexibility

Again, the theme is not optimization.
It is **protection**.

Health Savings Accounts (HSAs): The Quiet Powerhouse

For those eligible earlier in life, HSAs deserve special mention.

HSAs offer:

1. tax-deductible contributions
2. tax-deferred growth

3. tax-free withdrawals for qualified medical expenses—including long-term care

There is no other account with all three advantages.

Used patiently, HSAs can become a meaningful long-term care resource later in life.

Infinite Banking: Liquidity, Not a Silver Bullet

Infinite Banking uses a properly structured permanent life insurance policy to create:

- accessible liquidity
- predictable access
- flexibility during market downturns

The policy becomes a **tool**, not the goal.

For long-term care, this matters because expenses often arise:

- during market stress
- when simplicity is needed
- when liquidation would cause harm

Infinite Banking is not for everyone.
It requires discipline, time, and proper design.

It is best viewed as:

A liquidity layer—not a standalone plan.

Why No Single Strategy Stands Alone

Here is the most honest thing I can tell you:

Advanced planning works best when tools are coordinated.

That often means:

- a banker
- an estate attorney
- a CPA or tax strategist
- a wealth advisor
- an insurance professional

Each stays in their lane.
No one guesses.
No one sells in isolation.

Because bankers are not attorneys.
Attorneys are not CPAs.
And none of them should be improvising with
your future.

A Final Word on Ethics and Intent

Advanced strategies should never be used to:

- hide assets irresponsibly
- shift care costs unfairly
- create complexity without purpose

They should be used to:

- protect dignity
- protect a spouse
- reduce chaos
- preserve choice

The goal is not to outsmart the system.
The goal is to **navigate it wisely**.

Closing Reflection

Long-term care planning is not about fear.

It is about foresight.

The families who suffer most are not the ones who lacked resources.
They are the ones who lacked flexibility.

Advanced strategies exist because life is unpredictable.

Used thoughtfully, they don't eliminate hardship—but they **reduce harm**.

And in a system that often strips choice at the worst possible time,
that matters more than almost anything else.

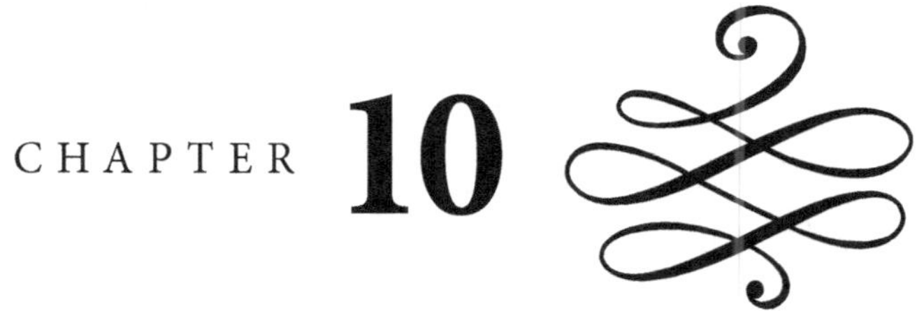

CHAPTER 10

The Workbook
The Just-In-Case Plan
A Practical Guide for Organizing What Matters Most

How to Use This Workbook

This workbook is not meant to be completed in one sitting. It is meant to be returned to—slowly, thoughtfully, and honestly.

You do not need perfection.
You need progress.

Each section stands alone, but together they form a master plan designed to:

- reduce stress
- prevent crisis-driven decisions
- protect dignity
- and make it easier for the people who love you to help when it matters most

If you complete nothing else, complete **Section 1**. Everything else builds from there.

Section 1: Access & Awareness

If nothing else, make sure this part exists.

Where are your most important documents stored today? *(Safe, filing cabinet, attorney's office, digital vault, fireproof box, etc.)*

____

____

Who knows how to access them if you cannot? *(List names and how they know where to look)*

____

____

What information would your family struggle to find quickly? *(Passwords, accounts, insurance, contacts, preferences)*

____

____

What conversations still need to happen? *(Be honest. This matters.)*

____

____

Section 2: Legal Foundation Checklist

☐ Will or Trust reviewed and current
☐ Beneficiaries reviewed and aligned with intent
☐ Medical Power of Attorney completed
☐ Financial Power of Attorney completed
☐ Living Will / Advance Directive completed
☐ Guardianship decisions considered (if applicable)
☐ Executor and trustees informed and willing
☐ Documents comply with current state law

Notes or updates needed:

____

____

____

Section 3: Financial Snapshot

This is not about net worth. It's about clarity.

Bank & Cash Accounts

☐ Checking ☐ Savings ☐ Money Market
Institutions & locations:

Retirement Accounts

☐ IRA ☐ 401(k)/403(b) ☐ Pension
Beneficiaries reviewed? ☐ Yes ☐ No

Other Assets

☐ Brokerage ☐ Real Estate ☐ Business Interests
☐ Annuities ☐ Cash-Value Life Insurance

What would confuse your family the most here?

____

____

____

Section 4: Insurance & Benefits

☐ Health insurance (Medicare, supplement, employer, ACA)
☐ Long-term care insurance (if applicable)
☐ Life insurance policies identified
☐ Annuities with LTC riders identified
☐ Veterans benefits explored (if applicable)

Policy numbers & contacts stored where?

____

____

____

Section 5: Medical & Care Preferences

☐ Primary care physician listed
☐ Specialists listed
☐ Medications documented
☐ Allergies documented

☐ Cognitive wishes discussed
☐ End-of-life preferences expressed
☐ Hospice preferences understood

What would you want your family to know if you couldn't explain it?

____

____

____

Section 6: Long-Term Care Reality Check

☐ Preferred care setting discussed (home, community, facility)
☐ Backup plans considered if preferred option is unavailable
☐ Financial impact discussed
☐ Spousal protection considered
☐ Caregiving expectations clarified

If care were needed tomorrow, what would be hardest?

____

____

____

Section 7: Family Roles & Sibling Coordination

Clarity now prevents conflict later.

Hold the Family Conversation Early

Sample opener:

"We all love Mom and Dad and want to do right by them. Can we talk about how to work together so no one carries the whole load alone?"

Who needs to be included?

____

Assign Roles by Strength (Not Birth Order)

☐ Paperwork & forms
☐ Appointments & errands
☐ Financial oversight
☐ Emotional support
☐ Technology & portals

Role assignments:

____

____

☐ Roles documented and shared
☐ Plan reviewed periodically

Fairness is not sameness.
Fairness is willingness.

Section 8: When Care Is Uneven Or Conflict Exists

Signs One Person Is Carrying Too Much

☐ Exhaustion ☐ Irritability ☐ Withdrawal ☐ Guilt
☐ Burnout

Supportive check-in:

"You're doing a lot. What can we take off your plate?"

If Siblings Cannot Work Together

☐ Keep communication factual
☐ Use written updates
☐ Define boundaries clearly
☐ Consider a neutral third party if needed

The goal is **safe, dignified care**, not perfection.

If You Are an Only Child

☐ Identify outside support early
☐ Build community resources
☐ Schedule respite
☐ Ask for help without guilt

Section 9: The "Third Base" Support System

The outside voice that helps keep peace.

☐ Trusted advocate identified
☐ No inheritance conflict

☐ Respected by parents
☐ Role clearly defined

Possible candidates:
☐ Family friend ☐ Banker ☐ Attorney ☐ Realtor
☐ Faith leader ☐ Senior advocate

Name & role:

____

____

____

Section 10: Advanced Strategy Awareness

(You do not need all of these. You need to know what exists.)

☐ Self-insuring assets identified
☐ IRA / tax exposure understood
☐ Medical deduction strategies discussed with a
professional
☐ Annuities with LTC riders understood
☐ Liquidity strategies identified
☐ Flexibility prioritized over perfection

What needs a second conversation?

____

____

____

Section 11: Your One-Page Strategy Map

What Must Be Protected

☐ Dignity ☐ Choice ☐ Spouse ☐ Home ☐ Relationships

Your Resources

☐ Income ☐ Assets ☐ Insurance ☐ Support people

Your Flex Points

☐ Where care happens
☐ Who provides care
☐ How care is funded
☐ What happens if plans change

Your biggest risk if you do nothing:

____

____

____

Section 12: Action Plan

One step you can take this month:

____

One conversation you've been avoiding:

____

Who should be part of the next conversation?

____

____

Master Completion Checklist

☐ Legal documents reviewed
☐ Financial accounts listed
☐ Insurance policies identified
☐ Medical preferences documented
☐ Trusted contacts informed
☐ Flexibility strategies understood
☐ Family conversations started

Final Note

Clarity is protection.
Planning is an act of love.

Avoiding the conversation does not spare your family—it burdens them.

You don't have to finish this today.
You just have to start.

© **Sherri L. Combs**
The Just-In-Case Plan

For a FREE downloadable copy of the workbook, scan the QR code in the back of this book. Or visit:
https://www.thejustincaseplan.com

Resources for Families Navigating Long-Term Care & Difficult Conversations

Because having support matters — and no one should walk this road alone.

Silver Streak Support & Services

Silver Streak Senior Services — Online Directory
A growing, user-friendly search platform designed to help seniors and families quickly locate **local, vetted service providers**, resources, and community support. This directory includes businesses that have undergone background, license, and insurance verification, so families can connect with trusted professionals more confidently. You'll also find links to many of the national and

community resources listed below — all in one place.
Website: https://*SilverStreakSeniorServices.com*

Silver Streak Senior Solutions — Public Charity

A nonprofit branch created to support seniors who may be struggling financially. In certain situations, **financial assistance may be available** for home repairs, mobility needs, safety upgrades, respite relief, or other essential aging-in-place support. Funding is based on need, availability, and board approval.
Website: *SilverStreakSeniorSolutions.org*

(These two sister-organizations work hand-in-hand — one connecting seniors to trusted help, the other lifting those who may not be able to afford it.)

Free & Low-Cost Community Resources

Area Agency on Aging (AAA)

Local branches offer support with benefits counseling, Medicare questions, caregiver planning, and education.
Search: *"Area Agency on Aging + your county/state"*

Senior Centers & Community Programs

Often provide support groups, legal clinics, social workers, and wellness checks.

Meals on Wheels

More than meal delivery — often includes safety visits and case management referrals.

AARP Caregiver Resources
Guides, workshops, and online tools for family planning.
aarp.org/caregiving

Caregiver Support & Education

Family Caregiver Alliance — caregiver.org
Alzheimer's Association — alz.org / 24-hr Helpline:
1-800-272-3900
Eldercare Locator — eldercare.acl.gov

Support groups, education, planning guides, and help understanding care options.

Professional Help (When a Neutral Guide is Needed)

Elder Law Attorneys — estate planning & future care decisions
Geriatric Care Managers — coordinate appointments & care plans
Family Therapists — support emotional healing & role reversal
Family Mediators — facilitate difficult conversations

Mediation can be extremely helpful when siblings disagree or decision-making stalls — but it can also be costly, so consider this option when communication alone isn't enough.

Technology & Tools to Coordinate Care

- Shared Google Drive or Dropbox folder
- Weekly family Zoom or group text thread
- Apps: CaringBridge, Lotsa Helping Hands, Medisafe, Abridge

Technology lightens the mental load and keeps everyone informed.

Practical Steps You Can Take Today

✔ Talk early — clarity is a gift to your future self
✔ Keep important documents accessible to more than one person
✔ Assign roles based on strengths, not birth order
✔ Check in regularly & share updates transparently
✔ Ask for help before burnout becomes resentment
✔ Remember — care is not meant to be carried alone

You Are Not Alone in This

Long-term care requires heart, patience, and support. You deserve resources that make this journey more manageable, hopeful, and human. Whether through **Silver Streak**, national organizations, or community programs, help exists — and every step toward planning now protects peace later.

NOTES:

This is my personal letter to you, Dear Older Ones,

Time seems to move so quickly now. One day blends into the next, and you find yourself wondering where it all went. You look around and ask yourself if anyone still sees you, if you still hold the same value you once did. The world feels louder, faster. People rush past you, their lives moving at a pace that feels unfamiliar. They run circles around you now. I know they do me too.

And yet—you still matter.

Throughout our lives, we carry many roles. We are builders, caregivers, providers, problem-solvers. We are captains of industry, pillars of our families, the steady hands others relied upon. We raised children. We helped shape our grandchildren when they were small and needed us in very tangible ways. Somewhere along the way, those roles began to change.

And when they do, a quiet question can creep in:

What do I have left to give?

Sometimes it feels like our usefulness has faded, as if value has an expiration date tied to productivity or speed. When the phone rings less often, when decisions are made without us, when our strength looks different than it once did, it can feel like we are no longer needed.

But here is the truth I want you to hear, and hear clearly:

Your value has never been tied to how fast you move, how much you produce, or how many people depend on you in obvious ways.

Your value lives in your perspective.
In your lived wisdom.
In the calm you bring simply by being present.

You have walked through storms others have not yet faced. You have survived seasons that once felt impossible. You hold stories, lessons, and insight that cannot be Googled or rushed. The world may not slow down enough to say it—but it still needs what only you carry.

You are not behind.
You are not invisible.
You are not finished.

This season of life is not about proving your worth—it is about recognizing it.

You may not always see the difference you are making, but that does not mean it is not happening.

Your grandchildren are watching more than you know. They notice how you speak to people, how you treat strangers, how you handle frustration, loss, and change. They are learning from you what it looks like to age with dignity.

The neighbors are watching too. So are their children. So are the people you pass in the grocery store. The cashier who looks like she is on the verge of tears. The man behind you who seems worn down by life. You notice these things because you have lived long enough to recognize them.

Your role has changed, but it has not disappeared.

Your role now is not to rush, produce, or prove anything.
Your role is to notice.
To offer kindness where it is missing.
To show patience where the world has forgotten how.
To remind the rest of us, by example, what decency, grace, and humanity look like.

Sometimes the difference you make is as simple as a kind word, a gentle moment, or a smile that says, "I see you."

Do not assume that your voice no longer matters.
Do not believe the lie that your usefulness has expired.
You are still shaping the world, just in quieter, deeper ways.

Do not ever tell yourself that no one wants to hear from an old woman or an old man. We do. We are living in a world that is starving for kindness, and you are one of its most reliable sources.

If you disappear, if you shrink back, if you hold yourself apart believing you no longer matter, then the rest of us lose something too. We lose the example of how to age gracefully. We lose the reminder of manners, patience, and kindness. We lose the living proof of what it means to remain human in a hurried world.

Whether we realize it or not, when we look at you, we are looking into a mirror of our own future. We are learning who we want to become.

In a world where we can be anything, I hope we choose to be kind.

And if no one has told you lately, let me be the one to say it:

You are still needed.
You are still valuable.
You are deeply seen.
And you are going to be okay.

A Letter to Caregivers
This is my personal letter to you.

Caregivers face unique challenges, and yet it is possible to meet those challenges and still hold onto your joy.

Some of you once longed to be empty nesters. Others loved the noise, the movement, the busy rooms filled with children and multiple generations. For some, a loud and bustling household felt like home. For others, you dreamed of a quieter season. A time when the kids were grown, the schedules eased, and you and your spouse could finally travel or simply rest after years of living by school calendars and responsibilities.

And then life changed.

Because of circumstances you did not plan for or expect, you became a caregiver.

You may have given up vacations. You may have stepped away from opportunities you once looked forward to. Your days may now be filled with doctor appointments that never seem to end. Your work life may suffer because your mind is often somewhere else, worrying about what is happening at home and how you are going to ask for yet another day off.

You may sit at your desk wondering if the stove was left on, if medications were taken, or if something unsafe was forgotten. These are not imagined fears. They are real, constant concerns.

Outwardly, you may smile and carry on. In private, you may find yourself giving way to tears.

Caregiving is an act of love, kindness, and deep self-sacrifice. Yet it is also often unseen. You may feel alone, especially if you are the first among your friends to walk this road. Others may not understand why you are less available, less spontaneous, or simply more tired.

Please hear this clearly.
You are not alone.

You *can* have joy, even in the midst of caregiving. Joy does not mean pretending this is easy. It means finding ways to steady yourself so you can continue with strength and compassion.

Burnout is real. Caregiving is emotionally draining. There are moments when you may feel you have nothing left to give. You may not have the energy to keep up with friendships or even respond to messages. You may go long stretches without proper sleep, much like caring for an infant, only now the responsibility feels heavier.

You may feel guilt for longing for freedom. Grief for the life you imagined. Frustration with yourself for moments when patience ran thin and words were spoken that you wish you could take back.

You may also be grieving the loss of the person your loved one once was. The vibrant, capable version of them that still lives in your memory.

And sometimes, you may feel taken for granted. The person you are caring for may be struggling with their own fear, grief, or loss of identity. Their pain may make it hard for them to express gratitude. That does not diminish your sacrifice.

Even if they never say thank you, others see you.
Your family sees you.
Your community sees you.

You are setting an example that reaches farther than you realize.

At some point, all of us will either give care or receive it. Caregiving is part of the human experience, across generations and circumstances. But none of us have unlimited energy. It is important to recognize your limits and to set boundaries. It is not failure to say no. It is wisdom.

You are not required to be a superhero. Accepting help does not mean you love your parent, spouse, or loved one any less. It means you understand that doing everything alone is not sustainable.

If someone offers to help, accept it without guilt. When you allow others to step in, you give yourself room to breathe, and you give your loved one the chance to build other connections as well.

Caregiving also requires discernment. Illness can change behavior, personality, and emotional regulation. Someone who was once gentle may become demanding, combative, or difficult. This is not a reflection of your failure. It calls for patience, grace, and compassion for both of you.

Do your best to care for yourself. Your physical health matters. Rest matters. Sleep matters. Even small moments of movement, quiet, or time outdoors can make a difference. You do not have to do this perfectly. Just try to do it gently.

Laughter matters too. Rarely does anything go exactly as planned. Finding moments of humor, even in frustration, can lighten the weight. If you can laugh together, it may strengthen your bond.

Stay connected to at least one person who understands or who listens without judgment. Choose wisely. Not every friend will know how to support you, and that is okay.

The season of caregiving is precious, even when it is hard. It is not forever.

I have a dear friend, Rebel Brown, who has been a caregiver to more people than I can count. She is writing a book called *Keeper of the Temple*, and that phrase captures something beautiful and true.

Your body is a temple. Something sacred.
And as a caregiver, you are a keeper of two temples.

Your role is sacred.

Each day, try to meet this role with dignity, patience, kindness, humor, and love. Your self-sacrifice is shaping lives in ways you may never fully see.

There are resources, support groups, and communities available to you. I have done my best to gather and share them through **Silver Streak Senior Services**, a platform created to bring trust, transparency, and support to caregivers and seniors alike.

It is a living, growing work. It will continue to evolve. And it is my gift to you. Use the code: CAREGIVERJICP and join for free.

You are doing meaningful work.
You matter.
And your care makes a difference.

Notes

Final Thank You

If you are holding this book, it means you were willing to pause.

Pause long enough to look ahead.
Pause long enough to ask hard questions.
Pause long enough to care—not just about yourself, but about the people who may one day have to step in for you.

That matters more than you know.

This book was written because I have seen what happens when families plan—and when they don't. I have sat with people at kitchen tables, in hospital rooms, in bank offices, and in moments of deep regret that could have been avoided with one honest conversation and one informed decision made sooner.

If this book helped you:

- start a conversation
- clarify a plan
- ask better questions
- or take even one step forward

then it has done exactly what it was meant to do.

You do not need a perfect plan.
You need a **living plan**—one that can adjust, evolve, and hold up when life does not go as expected.

Thank you for trusting me with a piece of your story. Thank you for caring enough to prepare.

And thank you, for the people who love you, and for whom you prepare for…you know…*just in case.*

— **Sherri L. Combs**